COMPREHENSIVE RESEARCH
AND STUDY GUIDE

E. E.
Cummings

BLOOM'S
MAJOR
POETS

EDITED AND WITH AN INTRODUCTION
BY HAROLD BLOOM

BLOOM'S MAJOR POETS

Maya Angelou

Elizabeth Bishop

William Blake

Gwendolyn Brooks

Robert Browning

Geoffrey Chaucer

Samuel Taylor Coleridge

Hart Crane

E.E. Cummings

Dante

Emily Dickinson

John Donne

H.D.

T. S. Eliot

Robert Frost

Seamus Heaney

A.E. Housman

Homer

Langston Hughes

John Keats

John Milton

Sylvia Plath

Edgar Allan Poe

Poets of World War I

Shakespeare's Poems & Sonnets

Percy Shelley

Wallace Stevens

Mark Strand

Alfred, Lord Tennyson

Walt Whitman

William Carlos Williams

William Wordsworth

William Butler Yeats

COMPREHENSIVE RESEARCH
AND STUDY GUIDE

E. E.
Cummings

CHELSEA HOUSE
PUBLISHERS
A Haights Cross Communications Company

Philadelphia

BLOOM'S
MAJOR
POETS

EDITED AND WITH AN INTRODUCTION
BY HAROLD BLOOM

© 2003 by Chelsea House Publishers, a subsidiary of
Haights Cross Communications.

A Haights Cross Communications ⬥ Company

Introduction © 2003 by Harold Bloom.

Printed and bound in the United States of America.

First Printing
1 3 5 7 9 8 6 4 2

Library of Congress Cataloging-in-Publication Data

E. E. Cummings / edited and with an introduction by Harold Bloom.
        p. cm.— (Bloom's major poets)
Includes bibliographical references and index.
    ISBN 0-7910-7391-2
    1. Cummings, E. E. (Edward Estlin), 1894–1962—Criticism and
interpretation. I. Bloom, Harold. II. Series.
    PS3505.U334Z59 2003
    811'.52—dc21

                                                    2003000806

Chelsea House Publishers
1974 Sproul Road, Suite 400
Broomall, PA 19008-0914
http://www.chelseahouse.com

Contributing Editor: Michael Baughan

Cover design by Terry Mallon

Layout by EJB Publishing Services

CONTENTS

USER'S GUIDE

This volume is designed to present biographical, critical, and bibliographical information on the author and the author's best-known or most important poems. Following Harold Bloom's editor's note and introduction is a concise biography of the author that discusses major life events and important literary accomplishments. A critical analysis of each poem follows, tracing significant themes, patterns, and motifs in the work. As with any study guide, it is recommended that the reader read the poem beforehand, and have a copy of the poem being discussed available for quick reference.

A selection of critical extracts, derived from previously published material, follows each thematic analysis. In most cases, these extracts represent the best analysis available from a number of leading critics. Because these extracts are derived from previously published material, they will include the original notations and references when available. Each extract is cited, and readers are encouraged to check the original publication as they continue their research. A bibliography of the author's writings, a list of additional books and articles on the author and their work, and an index of themes and ideas conclude the volume.

ABOUT THE EDITOR

Harold Bloom is Sterling Professor of the Humanities at Yale University and Henry W. and Albert A. Berg Professor of English at the New York University Graduate School. He is the author of over 20 books, and the editor of more than 30 anthologies of literary criticism.

Professor Bloom's works include *Shelley's Mythmaking* (1959), *The Visionary Company* (1961), *Blake's Apocalypse* (1963), *Yeats* (1970), *A Map of Misreading* (1975), *Kabbalah and Criticism* (1975), *Agon: Toward a Theory of Revisionism* (1982), *The American Religion* (1992), *The Western Canon* (1994), and *Omens of Millennium: The Gnosis of Angels, Dreams, and Resurrection* (1996). *The Anxiety of Influence* (1973) sets forth Professor Bloom's provocative theory of the literary relationships between the great writers and their predecessors. His most recent books include *Shakespeare: The Invention of the Human*, a 1998 National Book Award finalist, *How to Read and Why* (2000), and *Genius: A Mosaic of One Hundred Exemplary Creative Minds* (2002).

Professor Bloom earned his Ph.D. from Yale University in 1955 and has served on the Yale faculty since then. He is a 1985 MacArthur Foundation Award recipient and served as the Charles Eliot Norton Professor of Poetry at Harvard University in 1987–88. In 1999 he was awarded the prestigious American Academy of Arts and Letters Gold Medal for Criticism. Professor Bloom is the editor of several other Chelsea House series in literary criticism, including BLOOM'S MAJOR SHORT STORY WRITERS, BLOOM'S MAJOR NOVELISTS, BLOOM'S MAJOR DRAMATISTS, BLOOM'S MODERN CRITICAL INTERPRETATIONS, BLOOM'S MODERN CRITICAL VIEWS, and BLOOM'S BIOCRITIQUES.

EDITOR'S NOTE

My Introduction, a touch skeptical regarding the limitations of Cummings, nevertheless is an appreciation of "my father moved through dooms of love."

The early, rather Pre-Raphaelite "All in green went my love riding" is illuminated by the contrary readings of Barry Sanders and Will C. Jumper.

"Memorabilia," which I find problematic, is defended by all four Critical Views as a structure of allusions.

The robust "i sing of Olaf glad and big" requires no defense, but I particularly commend Gary Lane on the poem's inversion of classical values.

"somewhere i have never traveled, gladly beyond" is one of Cummings's most venturesome excursions into a metaphysic, and is examined as such in all three Critical Views.

"my father moved through dooms of love," Cummings's tribute to his formidable parent, is variously analyzed by the Contributing Editor, Michael Baughan, and in the five Critical Views. As my Introduction intimates, this seems to me as strong and interesting a poem as E. E. Cummings composed.

Harold Bloom

The poet's father, Edward Cummings, was by all accounts an impressive person: Unitarian minister, Harvard sociologist, an athlete and outdoorsman, an exuberant personality. He died in a locomotive-automobile collision in the autumn of 1926. "my father moved through dooms of love" was published as number 34 of the *50 Poems* (1934).

Any ambivalence between son and father overtly vanishes in this celebratory poem, though doubtless it remains between the lines, as it were. What renders this elegiac lyric so poignant is its identification with the dead father, and a wonderfully open expression of filial love:

> my father moved through dooms of love
> through sames of am through haves of give,
> singing each morning out of each night
> my father moved through depths of height
>
> this motionless forgetful where
> turned at his glance to shining here;
> that if(so timid air is firm)
> under his eyes would stir and squirm
>
> newly as from unburied which
> floats the first who, his April touch
> drove sleeping selves to swarm their fates
> woke dreamers to their ghostly roots
>
> and should some why completely weep
> my father's fingers brought her sleep:
> vainly no smallest voice might cry
> for he could feel the mountains grow.
>
> Lifting the valleys of the sea
> my father moved through griefs of joy;
> praising a forehead called the moon
> singing desire into begin

joy was his song and joy so pure
a heart of star by him could steer
and pure so now and now so yes
the wrists of twilight would rejoice

keen as midsummer's keen beyond
conceiving mind of sun will stand,
so strictly(over utmost him
so hugely)stood my father's dream

The characteristic flaw in Cummings is his flagrant sentimentalism, but who would find emotion in excess of the object in this poem? Hyperbolical flaws begin to appear after these first seven stanzas—"his anger was as right as rain" and "his shoulders marched against the dark." Still, the lively metric of the poem partly obscures these banalities. The two final stanzas are pitched so high that they ought not to work, but they do. The father, who preached the social gospel and believed in the potential divinity of all people, returns in the spirit to elevate the son's rhetoric:

though dull were all we taste as bright,
bitter all utterly things sweet,
maggoty minus and dumb death
all we inherit,all bequeath

and nothing quite so least as truth
—I say though that were why men breathe—
because my father lived his soul
love is the whole and more than all

Partly this is effective because Cummings is *not* his father: his own myth did not stress universal love, or potential divinity, but rather isolation, the difficulty of love, the reality of death. That makes more vivid and valuable the transcendence of his filial tribute.

E. E. Cummings

Edward Estlin Cummings was born October 14, 1894 in Cambridge, Massachusetts to parents of old New England stock. His father, Edward, was a professor of the newly created field of sociology at Harvard and later served as Unitarian Minister of the South Congregational Church of Boston. His mother, Rebecca, was a warm-hearted woman, much loved by adults and neighborhood children alike. Both encouraged Cummings's early interest in poetry and art, and continued to provide emotional and financial support whenever it was needed.

In 1899, the family bought Joy Farm, an idyllic retreat in the White Mountains near Silver Lake, New Hampshire where Cummings would spend nearly every summer for the rest of his life. The pastoral surroundings and good, country neighbors instilled in him a love of nature, simple pleasures, and humble, decent folk; all three became common themes in his poetry.

Cummings enrolled in Harvard in 1911 and focused his study on Classics and Literature, graduating *magna cum laude* four years later and staying on an extra year to earn his masters in English. He published his first poem in a 1912 issue of *The Harvard Monthly* and within a year was elected to serve on its editorial board with several like-minded peers. Among them were fellow writer John Dos Passos and two older, wealthier men, S. Foster Damon and Scofield Thayer, who were responsible for introducing Cummings to the writings of James Joyce, T.S. Eliot, and Ezra Pound as well as the artistic innovations of Impressionism and Cubism. Cummings's poetry at the time was quite conventional in style and content, displaying a clear debt to Keats and Dante Gabriel Rosetti. The sea change wrought by his exposure to modernist writers and painters is reflected in his 1915 commencement address, entitled "The New Art," as well as the four experimental pieces he selected for inclusion in *Eight Harvard Poets* (1917). These verses reveal Cummings' nascent fascination with the expressive potential of typographical arrangement and selective punctuation. They also contain his first use of the lowercase personal pronoun ("i"), a trademark of Cummings's work that symbolizes humility, his small physical stature, his poetic persona, and, most of all, the uniqueness of the individual. Tellingly, a copy editor corrected Cummings's "mistake" before the book went to press, presaging many misinterpretations to come.

After graduation, Cummings moved to New York and obtained his first and only job as a clerk for a mail-order bookseller. Three months later he quit and went to work full-time on his poetry and painting. In 1917, with Europe embroiled in war, Cummings volunteered for the Norton-Harjes Ambulance Corps. On the ship over to France he befriended William Slater Brown, a fellow pacifist. Ill-suited to the regimented life in the Corps, both were soon voicing their discontent in letters home. Brown's letters were particularly critical of the French war effort, and military censors began to question his loyalty. During an inquisition, Cummings defended his friend and refused to say he hated the Germans. Cummings and Brown subsequently spent four months in a detention camp before Cummings's father was able to use his contacts in the government to secure their release. Cummings recorded the experience in *The Enormous Room* (1922), an experimental prose work that remains one of the best pieces of war literature ever written by an American.

Drafted shortly after his return to the States, Cummings spent about six months at Camp Devens, Massachusetts. When the war ended, he moved back to New York, shared a studio apartment with Brown, and began painting and writing with renewed fervor. He entered several art exhibitions and published poems, line drawings, and a few prose pieces in *The Dial*, a literary magazine run by Scofield Thayer and J. Sibley Watson, another Harvard pal. During this period Cummings also began an affair with Thayer's wife Elaine that resulted in a daughter, Nancy. Elaine eventually divorced Thayer and married Cummings, but their union lasted less than a year and Cummings's daughter was not informed of her true parentage until she was nearly thirty years old.

Cummings spent the next decade splitting his time between Paris and New York. He published four poetry collections in quick succession: *Tulips and Chimneys* (1923), *&* (1925), *XLI Poems* (1925), and *Is 5* (1926). All received mixed reviews at best. His supporters at *The Dial* gave him an award for "distinguished service to American Letters," but many critics mistook his groundbreaking technique for deliberate obfuscation, reserving praise for only his traditional verses. Nevertheless, thanks to his unique style, satiric wit, and frank treatment of sexuality, he developed a small following and a reputation as a Greenwich Village iconoclast. In 1925 Cummings met Anne Barton, a spirited sometime fashion model who helped heal Cummings's heartbreak over Elaine. The two married in 1927. That same year, Cummings tried his hand at playwriting with *Him*, an uneven but fascinating exploration of artistic self-discovery with nearly two dozen scenes and three times as many roles. Produced by the Provincetown Players in 1928, it was praised by avant-garde critics and condemned by nearly everyone else.

1931 saw the publication of a collection of drawings and paintings, named *CIOPW* after the materials used (charcoal, ink, oil, pencil, and watercolor), as well as another volume of poetry, *W [ViVa]*. That same year, curious about Communism and state-sanctioned art programs, Cummings made a trip to Russia. An expanded version of his travel diary appeared in 1933, under the title *Eimi* (Greek for "I am"). Modeled on Dante's *Inferno*, it grimly depicts life under Party rule and, like *The Enormous Room*, celebrates the individual's ability to survive even the most oppressive conditions. With few exceptions, Cummings thereafter remained in the States, living at 4 Patchin Place in Greenwich Village and summering at Joy Farm. His marriage to Anne Barton had disintegrated in the early '30s, but his third wife, actress and model Marion Morehouse, proved a perfect match, and the relationship lasted the rest of his days.

In addition to two more dramatic pieces (*Tom*, in 1935, and *Santa Claus* in 1946) and a collection of essays (*A Miscellany*, 1958), Cummings continued to publish volumes of poetry at a rate of approximately one every four or five years. In his later works, he retains the same dazzling inventiveness with syntax and typography but leavens his satire with a transcendental vision of redemption and the regenerative power of love. The 1950s ushered in for Cummings a time of great popularity, public readings, exhibitions of his art, and overdue critical accolades. Fellowships from the Academy of American Poets (1950) and the Guggenheim Foundation (1951) were followed by the Charles Eliot Norton Professorship at Harvard in 1952–53. The last honor involved giving a series of public talks; published as *i: Six*

Nonlectures (1953), they provide a succinct and charming summation of his life and personal philosophy. Two years later he received a National Book Award citation for *Poems 1923-1954*, and two years after that he won the prestigious Bollingen Prize in Poetry from Yale University.

E. E. Cummings died of a brain hemorrhage at Joy Farm, on September 2, 1962. By then, the notion had already begun to circulate that his name should be written in all lowercase letters. The exact origin of this practice is unknown, but its entry into popular lore can be traced to the apocryphal assertion made by Harry T. Moore in the preface to Norman Friedman's *E. E. Cummings: The Growth of a Writer* (1964) that Cummings had his name legally lowercased, something his widow Marion Morehouse emphatically denied. Two recent articles by Friedman entitled "Not 'e. e. cummings'" and "Not 'e. e. cummings' Revisited" (published in *Spring: The Journal of the E. E. Cummings Society*) should have put the issue to rest, but certain publishers continue to perpetuate the myth. Whatever the "case" may be, there is no doubt that Cummings has attained a place of honor in the pantheon of American poets.

CRITICAL ANALYSIS OF

"All in green went my love riding"

Written while Cummings was still an undergraduate at Harvard and eventually published in *Tulips & Chimneys* (1923), "All in green went my love riding" presents a Cummings who has yet to turn his classical education into a tool for satire. The poem masterfully draws on the formulaic structure of oral poetry, the universal appeal and moral complexity of mythology, the symbolism of medieval allegory, the tonal beauty of the ballad, and the metaphoric connections between courtship and the hunt. It also illustrates the poet's early interest in infusing his verse with a highly visual, painterly aesthetic.

On its surface, the poem is a simple hunting narrative, comprised of fourteen distinct, detail-rich images like a stained glass window or medieval tapestry (see Lane for more on the latter). But what, exactly, is the storyline? We know from the last couplet that *something* falls "dead" at the end, but the pun on heart/hart (another word for a male red deer) leaves ambiguous whether the victim is a deer, the hunter, the narrator's affection, or some combination thereof. Contrary to charges leveled by his earliest critics, Cummings always left contextual clues for his readers, so what does the poem tell us about its external referents? Its use of repetition, tightly controlled meter, and personification (the bugle is "cruel," the arrow "famished") places it firmly in the tradition of oral epics. The singsong tonal quality, archaic diction, and the metaphor of the hunt all bring to mind a medieval ballad. Allegorical aspects are found in the highly suggestive color choices (the green hunter, the red deer, the gold horse, and the silver dawn) as well as the symmetry of the four hounds, does, and stags. As tempting as it might seem, it would be a mistake to interpret these subtle references to the Western canon as Cummings merely showing off his erudition or toying with his readers. Rather, by not directly naming his sources, he is encouraging reader participation and rewarding those who unearth literary analogs with a sense of discovery and personal engagement. The genres and traditions mentioned above all provide rich sources of insight into the poem. The greatest payload, however, is yielded by the myth of Diana and Actaeon.

The earliest version of the myth appears as a passing reference in Euripides, whom we know Cummings read at Harvard. In this version, the mortal Actaeon is torn to pieces by his own dogs after boasting that he was a better shot with a bow than Diana, virgin goddess of the hunt (Artemis, in Greek). In a later variant, recounted in Ovid's *Metamorphoses*, Actaeon happens upon Diana while she is bathing in a pool in the forest and does not hide his eyes. Diana turns the great hunter into a stag for his transgression, and he is chased and killed by his hounds. In the poem, Cummings does a little retelling of his own, developing a love affair from the romantic undercurrents contained in the bathing episode. This not only deepens the resonance of the hunting metaphor, but also broadens the possibilities for reader sympathy and interpretation.

The poem's diction helps determine who is Diana and who is Actaeon. The positive connotations of the alliterative phrases used to describe the deer ("swift sweet," "lean lithe," "sleek slim") and the negative connotations of the assonant phrases associated with the hunter ("cruel bugle," "famished arrow," and the "hounds crouched low") reveal the narrator's sympathy for the prey and antipathy towards the predator. In one of those morally ambiguous dualities so common in mythology, Diana was both goddess of the hunt and protectress of animals. It follows, then, that she is the speaker and Actaeon the hunter. This reading is further supported by several other textual elements. First, the introduction of "stags at a green mountain" towards the end of the poem suggests a foreshadowing of the metamorphosis by linking both the hunter and the stag with the color green (the color of spring, the season of change). Second, instead of advancing the plot or adding visual detail, the penultimate stanza's word for word refrain of the opening lines instills the expectation of a full circle return, thereby intensifying the shock of the transformation. Lastly, we have the now clarified meaning of the concluding pun: at the very moment he closes in on his quarry, as a song of triumph bursts from his lips, the hunter is transformed into a stag (or hart) and falls dead "before" his own hounds. Whether Actaeon deserves his fate is left an open question, as is the motivation and emotional state of the speaker. If she loves him, then why does she allow him to be killed?

Partial answers can be found in two of Diana's other aspects:

her chasteness and her vindictiveness. If the hunting metaphor is interpreted as a veiled bid for her maidenhood (the deer are "merry" as the chase begins and "tense" as it nears its conclusion, the hunter's bow is at his "belt"), then maybe more sense can be made of her treachery. Does her "heart" fall dead at the end because her virtue does not allow her to consummate the relationship? Or, conversely, is her heart broken and her ire unleashed by the discovery that her "love" was really only after her flesh? Then again, perhaps the simplest answer is the best: her love turned to anger when she saw how cruelly he chased the deer, and so she gave him a dose of his own medicine.

A familiarity with the myth of Diana and Actaeon can enrich our understanding of the poem; nevertheless, the poem does not succeed or fail based on the reader's knowledge of that specific myth. As most of the critical extracts following this analysis demonstrate, a more generalized reading allows for greater ambiguity about the genders of the speaker and the hunter, with quite varying interpretative results. The highly evocative but ultimately abstract subject matter, together with the poem's exquisite tonal and visual qualities, is what makes "All in green" as fresh and vital today as when it was first written. By the same token, knowledge of the poem's mythological basis does not steal its mystery.

Certain biographical details about the poet provide even more food for thought. In Richard Kennedy's *Dreams in the Mirror*, we are told that Cummings was an animal lover from his earliest years. We also learn that Edward Cummings, the poet's father, gave up hunting at the behest of his wife and took up nature photography instead. In a 1960 letter to Hildegard Watson, wife of lifelong friend J. Sibley Watson, Cummings wrote, "Well do I remember taking AJ ("Freddy") Ayer ... for a promenade near Joy Farm; during which stroll, my guest observed ... 'you're almost an animist, aren't you.' Quick-as-a-flash—withoutthinkingatall I deeply surprised myself by replying "'almost'? I AM an animist[.]" (*Selected Letters of E. E. Cummings*, p. 266) Though we can only speculate whether any of these things influenced the creation of the poem, and the work must ultimately speak for itself, there is fertile ground in the narrator's identification with the deer and the poetic justice of the surprise ending for anyone wishing to interpret the poem from an animist perspective.

"All in green went my love riding"

BARRY SANDERS ON THE ALLUSIONS TO DIANA

[Barry Sanders is a Professor of English at Pitzer College. He is the author of *A is for Ox: Violence, Electronic Media, and the Silencing of the Written Word*; *Sudden Glory: Laughter as Subversive History*; and *The Private Death of Public Discourse*. In this brief explication, he identifies many allusions to the goddess Diana and contends that she is the hunter in the poem.]

Little has been written about E. E. Cummings' poem "All in Green Went My Love Riding." The closest thing to a gloss of the poem is Alfred Kreymborg's comment in *Our Singing Strength* (New York, 1929). He suggests (p. 517) that there are "classical echoes" in the poem. I suggest that "All in Green Went My Love Riding" has more than mere echoes of classicism—it's directly concerned with the classical goddess, Diana.

Diana's principal function was goddess of the moon; thus it is not surprising to find that the woman in "All in Green Went My Love Riding" leaves when the dawn appears. One of Diana's secondary roles was goddess of the chase. As such she was frequently shown dressed in green ("All in green ..."), equipped with a hunting horn ("Horn at hip ..."), a quiver and bow ("Bow at belt ..."), and accompanied by hounds ("four lean hounds ..."). Further, all wild animals were sacred to her, but especially the deer, and Cummings has surrounded the woman in his poem with deer.

Since wild animals were sacred to her, Diana's chase was usually not associated with death. The death at the end of this poem, then, must have special meaning: the speaker dies only in his heart—he has fallen in love, perhaps with a Diana-like woman. But the speaker is without his woman at the end of the poem. Since Diana is traditionally a Virgin, she would know nothing of the joys and sorrows of love, and anyone under her aegis would be involved in a chaste, unrequited love. In this connection, we notice that the woman in the poem blows a "cruel" bugle. The *OED* gives these definitions for *cruel*: "indifferent to pain or distress," "destitute of compassion," "hard-hearted." At the same time, Cummings says that the woman is a "lucky" hunter, perhaps because, unlike the speaker, she will never know of love's sorrows, and, unlike the speaker, she will never be love's victim.

Placing "All in Green Went My Love Riding" in the volume where it first appeared in 1923, *Tulips and Chimneys*, we discover further justification for believing that Diana is the subject of this poem. The initial poem of *Tulips and Chimneys*, "Epithalamion," opens with a hymn to spring and closes with an invocation to the classical goddess, Venus. Cummings is combining a season with a classical deity. He may be continuing this strategy in "All in Green Went My Love Riding," for since Diana was also the goddess of the female productive powers in nature, we would assume her to be most active in the most "productive" season, the spring. (The green and gold imagery in the poem is not unlike the color imagery used to describe another vegetation deity, the Green Knight, in *Sir Gawain and the Green Knight*.) It seems logical, then, to assume that the speaker in Cummings' poem has his love interest aroused in that most "productive" season of love, the spring.

—Barry Sanders, "Cummings' 'All in green went my love riding,'" *The Explicator* 25, no. 3 (1966): Item 23.

WILL C. JUMPER ON THE FEMALE PERSONA

[Will C. Jumper is a Professor Emeritus of English at Iowa State University. In this rebuttal of Sanders, he argues that the narrator is female, the hunter male, and the basis of the poem medieval balladry.]

Barry Sanders' explication of Cummings' "All in Green Went My Love Riding" (EXP., Nov., 1966, xxv, 23) demonstrates the dangers of reading a poem without exploring the possible *personae* which the poet may have assumed for the purposes of the poem. Sanders' reasoning probably went thus: Edward Estlin Cummings wrote the poem; Cummings was a man; therefore the *persona* of the poem, the one who says "my," is a man.

If, however, Sanders had examined the fifteenth-century sources which inspired Cummings' poem, he would have realized that, regardless of the gender of the poet, the speaker of the poem might be female as well as male. In "All in Green," in fact, the *persona* is a woman. "My love" who went riding "all in green" is a man. No woman, in her daintiness, would ride "a great horse." The structure of the poem is not "cyclic" but is merely a sophisticated improvisation on the ballad pattern with repetition and repetition with variation throughout. (Sanders' reference to *Sir Gawain and the Green Knight* is extremely apt, but it argues exactly *against* his identification of the hunter with Diana.)

Furthermore, in Cummings' cunning use, "before" does not always mean "at a previous time (to)" or "in front (of)." In line 10, for example, it can have the older but still current meaning, "in the face (of) ," as it does, or can, in line 20 and line 30, and must in line 35.

In structure, then, the poem divides into the first five lines, which set the scene and define the refrain, and then into three groups of ten lines each, all of which are closed off by the refrain with variation, and all of which advance the "plot" incrementally. In lines 6–15, the green and silver promise of the first five lines is borne out. It's good hunting! That's why the hounds are smiling. The bugle is "cruel" at this point because it is indifferent to the distress of the quarry. It must be remembered that a medieval hunt was conducted not for *one* deer, but for enough game to "stock the larder." The hunter's retinue dressed the deer, or other game, fed the offal to the hounds, and sent the carcasses back, on the shoulders of their members, to be butchered for later cooking or preserving. In lines 16–25, the hunting is still good, but the hunter with his reduced retinue is advancing into more threatening territory—"the sheer peaks ran before"—where the game is more dangerous than the relatively easy kills at the "white water" and in the "level meadows."

This whole story is, of course, being reconstructed by the speaker of the poem, the "lady" back at the manor, who, perhaps, has received the kill from the earlier successes of the hunt. In lines 26–30, as in many old ballads, we get the threatening situation but not the climax. These deer of the mountains are "paler ... than daunting death" (these words were not chosen at random), and the hunter met "four tall stags." (Compare, in "Sir

Patrick Spens," the lines: "And I feir, I feir, my deir master, / That we will come to harme. // O our Scots nobles wer richt laith / To weet their cork heild schoone....") Up to this point, he was the "lucky hunter," and he "sang before," which is to say that he had sung previous to this confrontation, he sang before he attacked the four stags, and he sang in the face of his attack on them or their attack on him. But he became the ironic "lucky hunter" because one or all four of the stags gored him to death.

Lines 31–35, again like many old ballads, repeat the opening lines verbatim, with one fatal change, "my heart fell dead before," that is, in the face of this knowledge of the death of my love. The hounds are still smiling—they got their feast of blood one way or the other. But all that the *persona* of the poem now has to remember and to live with, even though her heart "fell dead," is that "All in green went my love riding / on a great horse of gold / into the silver dawn."

—Will C. Jumper, "Cummings' 'All in green went my love riding,'" *The Explicator* 26, no. 10 (1969): Item 2.

Cora Robey on the Predatory Instinct of the Female

[Cora Robey was a Professor of English at Tidewater Community College until her retirement in 1999. She has published articles on Baudelaire and Tennessee Williams in *Romance Notes*, and her *New Handbook of Basic Writing Skills* is now in its 5th edition. In this response to Sanders and Jumper, she sees a broader range of influences on the poem and suggests it is commenting on predatory aspects of the female.]

Professor Barry Sanders remarks on classical elements in E. E. Cummings' "All in Green Went My Love Riding" and suggests that the subject of the poem is the goddess Diana (EXP., Nov., 1966, xxv, 23. For an entirely different interpretation of the poem, see also that of Professor Will C. Jumper, EXP., Sept., 1967, xxvi, 6). While I think he is correct in seeing a strong classical element in the poem, his interpretation raises some questions which he is not entirely successful in answering. He stresses that deer were sacred to Diana and that Cummings has surrounded "my love" with deer, yet it seems quite clear from the poem that the deer are being pursued by the "four lean hounds crouched low and smiling" and finally become the victims of the "famished arrow." Sanders relates the fact that "my love" blows a "cruel bugle" and is a "lucky hunter" to her involvement with the speaker of the poem, suggesting that she is "lucky" in escaping love's sorrows; yet her luck more likely refers to her successful pursuit of the deer. Finally the green and gold imagery reminds Sanders of *Sir Gawain and the Green Knight*, a work which actually suggests a medieval rather than a classical frame of reference.

Perhaps these difficulties can be overcome by a less limiting interpretation of the poem. I feel that Cummings is making a comment about the predatory instinct of the female and that "All in Green Went My Love Riding," like many poems of Eliot and Pound, gains richness by relying upon several artistic traditions. Cummings borrows from the classical and medieval past and evokes the method of the Pre-Raphaelite poets in exploring his theme: the lover's vision of innate feminine cruelty.

The speaker is both viewer and commentator on the action; his comments reveal, in an understated way, his judgment of the scene. The hounds are "crouched low and smiling"; the bugle is "cruel"; the arrow is "famished"; all these observations suggest an avid, even a sadistic, pleasure taken in the chase and the kill. By contrast, the speaker's sympathies are clearly with the deer who are "merry" at the beginning of the poem and are described as "swift sweet," "red rare," "lean lithe," "fleet flown," and "tall tense," soon to be victims of the "famished arrow." The speaker's reference to the "lucky hunter" is ironic, since her success is the destruction of innocent majesty. The speaker's own reaction is contained in the last line: "my heart fell dead before." An awareness of the cruelty of "my love" which the speaker sees reflected in the sadistic pleasure shared by the hounds in the destruction of gentle and stately beauty causes his heart to fall "dead before."

The speaker's account suggests not only the classical deity Diana but also the cruel mistress of the courtly love complaint. "All in Green Went My Love Riding" is in the tradition of Troubadour poetry. In Guido Cavalcanti's "Voi, Che per Gli

Occhi Miei Passaste al Core," for example, the heart is slain by love. While in the Troubadour poetry, the speaker is unable to get outside of his own misery, however, Cummings' speaker is able to see the innate cruelty of his mistress by observing her in the company of the "four lean hounds." Finally, both the visual appeal of the poem and the use of the cruel-woman motif link Cummings with the Pre-Raphaelite poets. Rossetti's pictorial technique is suggested by Cummings in a series of tableaux: "Four red roebuck at a white water"; "Four fleet does at a gold valley"; "Four tall stags at a green mountain."

> —Cora Robey, "Cummings' 'All in green went my love riding,'"
> *The Explicator* 27, no. 10 (1969): Item 2.

WILLIAM V. DAVIS ON THE METAPHOR OF ROMANCE AND COURTSHIP

[William V. Davis is a Professor of English and Writer-in-Residence at Baylor University. His books of poetry include *One Way to Reconstruct the Scene*, which won the Yale Series of Younger Poets award, and *The Dark Hours*, which won the Calliope Press Chapbook Prize. He has also written several books of literary criticism, including *Understanding Robert Bly*. In this article excerpt, he focuses on the consequences of the female's innocence and naiveté.]

While I agree with the basic interpretations of this poem given by Sanders and Robey (and think that Jumper is rather wrong-headed), I would like to focus on the "greenness" of this "rider" and where it is she rides to, which is, I think, the clue to what Cummings was about in the poem. Certainly, the mistress is "cruel," as Robey says; but her "innate cruelty" is tempered by her "greenness"—her innocence, her naivete.

The poem is a metaphor about romance and courtship. For this reason Cummings does allude, as Sanders points out, to Diana, the goddess both of the moon and of the hunt or the chase. Cummings also plays on Diana's association with animals, the female reproductiveness in nature, and her virginity. All of these allusions to Diana are obvious and even explicit in the poem and her "greenness" applies to most of them, most specifically, of course, to her virginity. The "lady" pursues the narrator through the throes of a romantic courtship *via* the metaphor of the chase of which Diana, as huntress, is "goddess." In the chase the "lady" takes the role of pursuer, the lover that of pursued. The chase traverses the differing emotions of the landscape of courtship. In references such as "the level meadows ran before" and "the sheer peaks ran before" we see the joys and sorrows, the pleasures and disappointments of a courtship. (In this regard the several references to the deer, who, in terms of the chase metaphor is of course the hunted animal, come to be possible allusions to the lover, the hunted man, if we think of this word in terms of its etymology—both deer and dear derive from the Old English deor.)

And the lover is willing to play the game for what it is worth. Finally, however, when the prey is at bay ("Four tall stags at a green mountain / the lucky hunter sang before"), the "lady's" innocence, her "greenness," presents problems. She is, on the one hand, "lucky" in that she has caught her lover and now has him in her grasp; but, on the other hand, her "luck" must be seen as ironic in that, having caught her prey, she doesn't know how to handle the situation because of her innocence, her "greenness." At this point in the romance and after the playfulness of the pursuit by the "lady," the lover should be ready to assert himself with respect to her pursuance in some direct way. She, seeing this, and not knowing how to cope with it, in her fear and innocence, kills him ("my heart fell dead before").

It seems significant that the setting of the poem is "the silver dawn." Literally, this time of day would apply explicitly to a hunt, which usually takes place (or begins) in the early morning, about dawn. The time of day also pertains to the Diana figure, especially (in "silver") as moon goddess. But metaphorically the "silver dawn" is even more interesting. Dawn is a twilight time, a time of change. The twilight of "dawn" refers to morning, when from out of darkness comes light. Metaphorically then, and in terms of the theme of the poem as I nave suggested it above, Cummings would appear to be saying, in a very subtle way, that the "lady" of the poem, most ironically, cannot enter the world of daylight with respect to love. Rather she remains in the dark and, because she cannot make the transition to mature (married?)

love, must finally "kill" her lover. Cummings implies that these things don't even "dawn" on the "lady."

The final question then is the meaning of the last line of the poem. In keeping with the theme of the poem as I see it, it would seem to be obvious that in the line, "my heart fell dead before," Cummings, or the narrator, is referring not to a literal death but rather to a metaphoric death which applies to the courtship theme. This symbolic or metaphoric death can be viewed as the death of the narrator's interest in his "lady" because of her naivete with respect to the love and courtship relationship and of what it might lead to. The "lady" must kill her lover in order to disguise her frigidity, her inability to accept a mature relationship.

> —William V. Davis, "Cummings' 'All in green went my love rid-ing,'" *Concerning Poetry* 3 (1970): 65–67.

IRENE R. FAIRLEY ON SYNTACTIC DEVIANCE

> [Irene R. Fairley is a Professor of English at Northeastern University. Her other publications include "Millay's Gendered Language and Form" (*Style*), and a chapter from *Twentieth-Century Fiction: From Text to Context* (1995) entitled "Virginia Woolf's Old Mrs. Grey: Issues of Genre." This extract from her book on Cummings's unorthodox use of grammar explains how Cummings's use of "deviance" is patterned in the poem.]

[In Cummings' "All in green went my love riding"] deviance and regularity are yoked within the syntactic pattern for each stanza. Four syntactic patterns, each characterized by a major displacement, are the basis for a cyclical stanzaic structure.[7] (...)

The pattern introduced in the first stanza is characterized by V/S inversion, "went my love," and phrasal modifiers in initial and terminal positions. In its second instance the initial modifier "All in green," which derives from a sentence such as *she was dressed all in green* that is embedded as a sentence adverbial and then reduced, is varied to "Horn at hip." The surface pattern and embedding process is preserved with a change in token, while the underlying structure of the modifier is varied to, perhaps, *she had a horn at her hip*. The complement extends into line 3 replacing the manner adverbial, and the second adverbial is repeated exactly. The initial sentence pattern is not radically altered, all changes are minor. In the third instance Cummings follows the revised pattern varying only the surface tokens: *bow* replaces *horn*, and *mountain* replaces *echo*. The original pattern is repeated exactly in the fourth and last instance in stanza 13.

In the second stanzaic pattern the lines are simply reversed, the object of the preposition occurs in initial rather than its standard terminal position. The syntactic shift generally corresponds to our sense of spatial relationships if we imagine the hunt in conventional terms as a left to right sequence; the deer are running before the hounds. The displacement increases a sense of action in another way. Reading the first line one is likely to assign the syntactic values of NP–V–Adv until arriving at "and smiling" which forces us to consider the sentence as a whole, and to reevaluate the first line as object of the preposition, as a noun phrase with a reduced relative clause modifier. The inversion, thus, creates a dual reading of the two lines, as both a series of actions, and as a statement of spatial relationships. But the two are conceptually interdependent. The first reading in which "crouched" is assigned a + *verbal* feature can be considered in generative terms an early stage in the derivation of the final surface structure. The shifted object is repeated exactly all four times, while the subject token varies in the second the third instances to "the level meadows" and "the sheer peaks." A significant change occurs in the fourth instance, in the line which ends the poem, as the S–V varies to "my heart fell dead."

The third stanza pattern parallels the first; also having three lines, it forms an antithetical correspondence of hunter/hunted. It too has the V/S inversion, and the dislocation of the adjectival predicate creates a similar effect of the S and V surrounded by modifiers. The series of appositive noun phrases which function as adjectival modifiers correspond to the adverbial modifiers of the first pattern. The third pattern does not fluctuate syntactically, only lexical tokens change; *fleeter, softer, paler; dappled dreams, slippered sleep, daunting death; swift sweet, lean lithe, sleek slim; red rare, fleet flown, tall tense.*

The fourth stanza pattern corresponds to the second, having

two lines, the same syntactic shift, with an antithetical referent, and a reversal of modification—this time adverbial rather than adjectival. As with the third pattern, there are no structural changes, only variations of tokens.

The poem is highly structured. Stanzas of the first and third patterns advance the descriptive level of the poem, the second and fourth advance the action, plot. There are several levels of correspondence: of reference, number of lines in a stanza, and of syntactic pattern; linked in a complex pattern of alternating and corresponding stanzas. These correspondences are further reinforced by lexical and phonetic repetitions.

The effect is lyrical, perhaps too lyrical for contemporary taste which tends toward the prosaic. The parallelism, degree of correspondence, may seem excessive. Though each pattern involves major shifts, rearrangement rules correspond. As set forth in Chapter V, rules (1) and (2) operate in stanzas one and three, rule (1) in stanzas two and four; the repetition of the pattern diminishes the sense of deviance, irregularity, and the V/S inversion is traditional to poetry. Even a syntactically deviant pattern can become redundant.[8]

The poem, however judged, does illustrate a form of parallelism in which the deviance is an integral part of the pattern, rather than a variation to it.

NOTES

7. Two interpretations of this poem have appeared. B. Sanders in *The Explicator*, XXV (November, 1966), 23, describes the speaker as an unrequited lover whose heart is captured by the classical goddess, the huntress Diana, and mentions a cyclical, seasonal structure. Will C. Jumper in *The Explicator*, XXVI (September, 1967), 6, has taken issue with Sanders' interpretation, insisting that the gender of the speaker is female, that the speaker recounts in courtly fashion the tale of her lover's fatal hunt. He argues that "the structure of the poem is not 'cyclic' but is merely a sophisticated improvisation on the ballad pattern with repetition and repetition with variation throughout." I agree with Sanders' and hold to a male speaker and figurative hunt, but the identification of gender is not crucial to my analysis. It is necessary, however, to recognize the play of a sexual or binary opposition. Also, both observations regarding the structure of the poem would seem to have validity, and are supported by the following discussion of two related stanzaic systems and the structural complexity of the poem.

Philip J. West, "Medieval Style and the Concerns of Modern Criticism" (*College English*, 34, March 1973), presents an analysis of this poem from oral-formulaic premises.

8. Parallelism indicates functional selection of generative rules. Many of Cummings' parallelisms can be explained as repeated applications of the optional rules set forth in Chapter V.

—Irene R. Fairley, *E. E. Cummings and Ungrammar: A Study of Syntactic Deviance in his Poems*, (New York: Watermill Publishers, 1975): 130–134.

Gary Lane on the Poem as a Medieval Tapestry

[Gary Lane is the author of numerous books on poetry, including *Sylvia Plath: New Views on the Poetry*, *A Concordance to the Poems of Dylan Thomas*, and *A Concordance to Personae: The Shorter Poems of Ezra Pound*. In this excerpt from his book on Cummings, he identifies the poem's foundation as the myth of Diana and Actaeon and discusses how it is structured like a medieval tapestry.]

Cummings studied classical languages at Harvard, but like Ezra Pound, whom he knew and admired, he spoke often in his poems the medieval tongue of courtly love. Nowhere does he weave more gracefully these threads ancient and merely old than in the verbal tapestry "All in green went my love riding." This luminous, initially perplexing poem is at last a statement by example of one of Cummings' fundamental aesthetic beliefs. Fusing the Diana and Actaeon legend with the medieval hunt, bringing the resources of ballad and allegory to a uniquely expanded Shakespearean sonnet, the poem gathers at the intersection of beauty and terror. From the emotional vantage point of that crossing—the poet achieves it through fourteen haunting tableaux, each at once distinct and implicative—we can infer a good deal about the essence of tragedy and beauty, the nature of passivity and action.

Myth enwrought seems substance here, the subject a lover's dilemma. In Roman (and Greek) mythology, Diana (Artemis), chaste goddess of the chase, protectress of wildlife, is challenged by Actaeon, a famous but mortal hunter who feels he can outshoot her. The goddess, whether directly for his ὕβρις or because Actaeon is indeed the better marksman, changes him into a stag. He feels fear for the first time, and his hounds, sensing this, set upon and kill him. Adding romance to the myth—a courtly Diana here, loving the hunter, is torn between the gentle beauty of the deer and the chivalric flash of their pursuer—Cummings intensifies the fatal transformation toward which the action builds.

This poem is evidence—more profound evidence, I think, than Cummings' celebrated quasi-ideograms—that the painting side of the man lived always with the poet. Dramatically visual, "All in green" suggests in its use of myth, its courtliness, and its spatial orientation a medieval tapestry. Each stanza is not merely self-contained—unusual for Cummings—each is primarily a picture. Thus we see emphasized the physical characteristics of the action—number, color, place—rather than the actors' states of mind. Thus, too, the word "before," ending seven of the fourteen stanzas, recurs: it offers visual perspective, the graphic layout. The painter's specificity, then, encompasses not merely concrete details, though these abound, it extends as well to composition; we see not only "four red roebuck at a white water" and the "cruel bugle," synecdochic hunter, but are shown also the relative positions of the antagonists, watering deer to the right, hunter at the left foreground. The whole technique is particularly useful in this poem because its frame effect, the suspense-creating discontinuity that forms and informs tapestry, leaps sudden as a clicked shutter to the hero's unexpected death.

Graphically conceived, the poem is nevertheless linear in structure. Its literal magic is prefigured and given context by the echo of ballad and allegory—by repetition and the miraculous, pregnant detail and narrative enigma—and its poetic magic owes still more to the tightness of the Shakespearean sonnet. Indeed, if we consider each stanza an extended single line, "All in green" *is* such a sonnet. Thus we may divide it into three minutely parallel "quatrains" and a final, surprising "couplet." Told from Diana's point of view, the poem in its quatrains develops the increasingly difficult chase and presents the convergence of the speaker's conflicting sympathies; its couplet concentrates the fatal metamorphosis into a fine and final pun.

Specific lines offer little difficulty. Shortly after a courtly start—the "green," "gold," and "silver" of expanded line 1 might fancifully suggest medieval illumination—the poem becomes ominous with suggestive conflict. Line 2, juxtaposing odious hounds and "merry deer," sets sympathies as well as sides; line 3 underscores them. When "my love" is identified as a hunter by the "cruel bugle" of line 4, the dilemma's horns begin to sprout. With the second quatrain—the "horn at hip" is of course the preceding line's bugle—the hunt quickens. Ground shifts from "a white water" to "level meadows" and "a gold valley"; Diana's description of the deer trades the lightness of "dream" for more serious "sleep." No mere bugle now, the equipment of the chase is "the famished arrow." The final quatrain brings to a climax both chase and dilemma. The ground rises to "sheer peaks" and "a green mountain"; the tired deer, now within range, are "paler ... than daunting death."

Yet the "lucky hunter" is attended by a complex irony that prefigures disaster. If he is lucky in anticipated success, it is that very success which will undo him. If he is lucky in the medieval sense of affection—"Ye gaif me lief, fair lucky dame" (OED)—at this crucial moment he will prove insufficiently dear to Diana. There is, then, a simple verbal irony too: for the couplet, cryptically spanning the hunt from start to finish—its first line repeats the poem's first—springs the news of Actaeon's death. Changed by the goddess into a hart, a red male deer, he is killed by his dogs. And so the final cry, "my heart fell dead before," concentrates Actaeon both as Diana's love and as metamorphosed deer, while conveying at the same time the lady's terrified swoon.

The implication of this allegoric hunt, the upshot of this mixture of sonnet and tapestry, linear exposition and graphic concept, lies in the poem's movement. From the outset we are caught in a dreamlike flux of color, landscape, even gender. In the half-light of dawn, "green," "gold," "silver," "red," and "white" flash past. Terrain alters, and even the deer change from "roebuck" to "does" to "stags." Static in this flux, an insistent refrain repeated once for each dog, are "four lean hounds crouched low and smiling." Unmoving, uncolored, they can kill others, but as Yeats, "a true poet" (L 188), had taught, they are themselves dead. For if

> The horse that comes from the road,
> The rider, the birds that range
> From cloud to tumbling cloud,
> Minute by minute they change,

then these hounds, perpetually still in the midst of all, contradict the life-defining principle of kinesis.

Ultimately, "All in green" asserts the superiority of action to pulse-beat, dying to death-in-life. Diana and Actaeon both suffer a kind of death, but because their losses are sustained in passion rather than passivity, those deaths are life-giving. Literally, of course, their tragedy saves the deer; classically, however, and in the tradition of the sonnet, it perpetuates the lovers themselves, making their story memorable and fit for poetry. Cost what it must, Cummings tells us, action alone proves vital; in the vacuum of its absence, love—life—is sucked away. There is, then, beauty in tragedy, though a terrible beauty, because tragedy is active. Only the hounds here, crouched and colorless, neither move nor move *us*; stasis alone, in the world of E. E. Cummings, is immitigably ugly.

—Gary Lane, *I Am: A Study of E. E. Cummings' Poems*, (Lawrence: The University Press of Kansas, 1976): 60–63.

CRITICAL ANALYSIS OF

"Memorabilia"

Filled with intentionally jumbled literary and cultural references, verbal parody, and comic fatalism, "Memorabilia" (*is 5*, 1926) is a biting satire on tourism, especially as practiced by uneducated Americans in organized groups, who hit all the highlights without absorbing anything in depth. It is also a good example of the way Cummings uses unorthodox syntax to achieve his aesthetics ends.

Cummings made frequent visits to the Continent throughout much of his life, and even resided in France for two separate, extended periods of time. Thanks to his classical training at Harvard and innate talent for languages, he made an effort to speak the local tongue wherever he went (he was quite fluent in French). He also became acquainted with fellow poets and painters, patronized the local arts, sketched his impressions, and otherwise engaged and absorbed as much as possible. His first trips abroad (during WWI as part of the Norton-Harjes ambulance corps and several years later, with friend and fellow writer John Dos Passos) were at a time when Europe was virtually devoid of tourists. That began to change in the postwar years and by 1926, when the poem was written, Cummings was evidently fed up with the influx, "particularly the / brand of marriageable nymph which is / armed with large legs rancid / voices Baedekers Mothers and kodaks."

Cummings's poems rarely have titles beyond their opening lines, so when one is present it merits special attention. In this case, "Memorabilia" recalls both its standard dictionary meaning and the Robert Browning poem of the same name—a meditation on how experiences, however vividly remembered, lose their meaning when robbed of context. The narrator in Browning's poem uses two memories as examples. First, an unnamed person recollects running into Percy Shelley on the street. To the narrator (Browning), it is the event of a lifetime. To the unnamed person, it is of little consequence and he laughs at the narrator's awe. Next, the narrator remembers finding an eagle feather but can recall nothing about the moor where he found it. By alluding to Browning's poem, Cummings is not only parodying (in a self-deprecating manner) the tradition of invoking poets past, he is also advancing Browning's point by suggesting that memory itself can be guilty of being a tourist.

The opening imperative in Cummings's poem, "stop look & / listen," evokes both the safety slogan posted at railroad crossings (here a warning against the masses of tourists to come) and the directions a tour guide would give to his or her otherwise clueless followers. In an ironic role reversal, the words are not directed at the tourists but at three commonly visited sites in and around Venice: the "glassworks of Murano," the "elevator" of the Campanile, and the crocodile ("cocodrillo") that forms part of the statue of St. Theodore near the Piazza San Marco. The next four words, "Venezia: incline thine ear," give the setting for the poem and introduce the first instance of elevated diction, a device used throughout to mimic the empty rhetoric of the tourists and their guides. Does Cummings choose "Venezia" over "Venice" in deference to the Italians, in a satirical comment on tourists who use snippets of a foreign tongue to give themselves an air of sophistication, or simply for its melodious sound? Given Cummings's penchant for multiplicity, any or all three are likely. "Incline thine ear" is also the first of two Biblical references, used throughout the scriptures to emphasize a given lesson or truth.

The next few lines introduce the aforementioned sites addressed by the narrator. They also include two more allusions. The first ("nel / mezzo del cammin'") is from the opening lines of Dante's *The Divine Comedy* and means in the middle of the road or journey, not "half-way up the Campanile" as Cummings playfully mistranslates it. The second ("mine eyes have seen / the glory of / the coming of") is from "The Battle Hymn of the Republic" and suggests a militaristic, perhaps even imperialist, aspect to the tourist takeover.

Dropping the names of popular promenades ("Riva Shiavoni") and expensive hotels ("de l'Europe Grand and Royal / Danielli") further parodies the behavior of the tourists. Likening their numbers "unto the stars of Heaven..." (the second Biblical reference) recalls, and perhaps questions the wisdom of, the angel's promise to multiply Abraham's progeny after he proves his faith with his willingness to sacrifice Isaac.

The following stanza uses repetition, slant rhyme, and

disjointed word order to add aural texture to the scene and further drive home the damage done by the presence of tourists. The once charming gondoliers sound like carnival barkers with their incessant, interrupting entreaties, especially when the stanza climaxes with the jarring collision of "Cincingondolanati" —a pseudo-Italian neologism that brings to mind a tacky theme park. The ridiculous rhyming of "gondola" with "Omaha," and "Altoona," hits another dead end at "Duluth." The only thing these culturally vacant Midwestern cities can offer Venice is their overweight "dollarbringing" daughters.

The confusion increases in the penultimate stanza, as the poem devolves into a cacophony of sound bytes, almost Cubist in its fragmented depiction of the many-headed horde. The "Loggia" refers to the balcony of St. Mark's Basilica, which overlooks a typically crowded plaza. "Ruskin says" refers to John Ruskin, the nineteenth century art critic and author of the classic travelogue *The Stones of Venice*. The final tragedy of this stanza is that in the end, presented with a city full of architectural and artistic wonders, the tourist can think of nothing to say but "isn't this wellcurb simply darling."

The following line contains another literary allusion as well as a good example of Cummings's talent for typographical nuance. The piling up of apostrophes ("O Education," "O Thos cook & son," "O to be a metope") parodies a Latin poet calling on a muse or deity for help. Quite possibly, Cummings is also referencing a specific line from Cicero's speech against Catiline—"O times, O customs"—in which the great orator decries the general state of affairs. Putting "O Education" way out at the right margin reemphasizes what the tourists are lacking. Bracketing "Education" with two "O"s graphically depicts the metope mentioned in the second to last line (see below). Though Cummings has never been credited with the invention, one could also see in the dismayed, gape-mouthed face created by the colon and second "O" a precursor of the "emoticons" commonly used today in email correspondence.

"Tho[ma]s cook & son," is an extremely successful travel firm that organized some of the first tours of the Continent. Invoking its name in this context is an implicit indictment, for its contribution to the culture of tourism and the subsequent degradation of once great cities like Venice.

The final couplet gives the reader one last metaphor to mull over. It also bookends the poem with another allusion to Browning, who, readers should note, died in Venice. Echoing the homesick opening lines of "Home Thoughts, from Abroad" ("O to be in England / Now that April's there"), the narrator wishes he were a metope, "now that triglyph's here." In Doric friezes (decorative horizontal bands that appear above columned façades), metopes are the panels between sets of three vertical bands in relief (triglyphs). What makes Cummings's metaphor so ambiguous is that these panels can either be blank or filled with (often brightly painted) bas-relief sculptures. Triglyphs, on the other hand, are always the same; they serve to highlight and frame what comes between them. So either the narrator wants to blend into the background or else be the artistic variable among unchanging homogeneity. Regardless, the narrator is once again contrasting himself from the tourists.

After painstakingly parsing out many of the hidden references and inside jokes of the poem, one can't help wondering whether Cummings is being deliberately cryptic and, if so, extending to his less erudite readers the same elitist scorn that he shows for the tourists. It certainly would not be the first time he was charged with such a crime. However, when dealing with Cummings, readers should always be cautious about stopping at surface-level impressions. Invariably, there is a method at work— an attempt to engage and involve the reader. Although there is a certain degree of intellectual and cultural arrogance in the tone of the poem, Cummings would never intentionally alienate his readers. As he explains in his foreword to the first edition of *Collected Poems*, "the poems to come are for you and for me and are not for mostpeople—it's no use trying to pretend that mostpeople and ourselves are alike. Mostpeople have less in common with ourselves than the squarerootofminusone. You and I are human beings; mostpeople are snobs."

"Memorabilia"

CLYDE S. KILBY ON LITERARY AND CULTURAL ALLUSIONS

[Clyde S. Kilby was a Professor of English at Wheaton College from 1935 until his retirement. His other publications include *Poetry and Life: An Introduction to Poetry* and *The Christian World of C. S. Lewis*. Here he explicates many of the subtle references in the poem.]

This poem (*Collected Poems*, 138; 1938) is obviously a satire on American tourists, particularly "marriageable nymphs," armed not only with the usual Baedekers and kodaks but in this instance with hopeful mothers, all of them "seeing" Italy on a professionally organized tour. The title itself is satiric, alluding not only to the ordinary meaning of "memorabilia" as "things worthy of being remembered" but also perhaps to Browning's poem of that name beginning "Ah, did you once see Shelley plain?" and expressing surprise that one could survive the emotional shock of such an experience.

The tourists are as omnipresent as the stars of Heaven. The gondolier, calling out dollar-wise for customers (lines 22–28), is cynical about the noisy flow of "denizens" above and below him. Lines 36–36 present the tourists following a professional guide who quotes Ruskin and describes art treasures to them while they chatter. Gondoliers and guides seem to know the whole thing is only skin-deep and go through their motions mechanically.

Interspersed throughout are quotations from a variety of sources. The poem begins with the American safety slogan "Stop, look, and listen"—here a call for all things Italian to pause, even the elevator half-way up the Campanile, and hear the oncoming Americans. The second quotation (lines 10–12) is from the "Battle Hymn of the Republic" and suggests the endless tramp, tramp of the army of tourists. "By night" probably alludes to Longfellow's account of Paul Revere's ride and again suggests danger ahead. Two other fragments are from the Bible: "Incline thine ear" and "Their numbers are like unto the stars of

Heaven." Both expressions are frequent in the Scriptures, the former calling for special attention to be given to some particular truth and the latter describing the multitude of children promised to Abraham. The dignity and elegance of these expressions contrast with the irony of their meaning in this poem. The last two lines recall the opening of Browning's poem written in Italy, "Oh, to be in England / Now that April's there." "Metope" and "triglyph" are architectural terms and describe a portion of a Doric frieze, the metope being the decorated section between triglyphs. Perhaps the poet is saying that one beautiful thing—the tourists—deserves another—the art treasures of Europe, endlessly.

—Clyde S. Kilby, "Cummings' 'Memorabilia'," *The Explicator* 12, no. 2 (1953): Item 15.

CYNTHIA BARTON ON THE POEM'S STRUCTURAL ORGANIZATION

[Cynthia Barton is a writer and educator. She has written several articles for *Cobblestone Magazine*, and the Orchard House publication, *Portfolio*. She is also the biographer of Clara Endicott Sears and a regular lecturer at the Bronson Alcott School of Philosophy in Concord, Massachusetts. In this response to Kilby, she postulates that the poem's three main sections are comprised of responses by the tourist sites to the opening injunction "stop look & listen."]

I would like to add a few remarks to Clyde S. Kilby's explication of Cummings' "Memorabilia" (EXP., Nov., 1953, xii, 15). Although he properly comments upon the satirical tone and identifies many of the literary allusions, he fails to recognize the basic structural organization of the poem. The form is derived from the phrase "Stop look & / listen." The opening invocation calls upon three elements of the city of Venice to obey the injunctions, and the three sections which follow are the responses to these commands.

Cocodrillo, a large stone crocodile which is part of a statue of St. Theodore on a tall column overlooking the Piazza San Marco, is ordered to look. His section (lines 10–21 and line 29) is a visual image ("mine eyes have seen / the glory") of the invading army of "substantial dollarbringing virgins." He describes their appearance ("large legs") and their various equipment ("Baedekers Mothers and kodaks"). He sees them as they crowd the bank of the Grand Canal and swarm around the region of best hotels in numbers "like unto the stars of Heaven." In the second descriptive section (lines 22–28) the elevator which has been ordered to stop "mezzo del cammin" obeys the command. It "affirms"—does not "see" or "hear"—that the "denizens of Omaha Altoona or what / not" pass "loudly" and "rapidly" "above" and "below." This passage is a kinesthetic image of the tourists in motion given by the elevator which has temporarily ceased to move. The words "gondola" and "signore" are inserted, as Ben W. Griffith, Jr., states (Exp., May, 1954, xii, 47), "as a contrapuntal theme to demonstrate the sounds of the city—more specifically the shouts of the gondoliers." They also, as Mr. Kilby suggests, serve to emphasize a contrast in sound between Italian words and the harsh names of the American cities. The third section completes the picture of the tourists by presenting the aural image received by the "inclined ear" of the usually noisy "glassworks of Murano." Their voices are heard mingled with the spiel of a professional guide.

—Cynthia Barton, "Cummings' 'Memorabilia'," *The Explicator* 22, no. 4 (1963): Item 26.

H. SETH FINN ON PARALLELS WITH T. S. ELIOT'S "THE LOVE SONG OF J. ALFRED PRUFROCK"

[H. Seth Finn is an Associate Professor of computer and information systems and communications at Robert Morris College. He is the author of a number of publications, including *Broadcast Writing as a Liberal Art*. Here he presents evidence for the poem's debt to T. S. Eliot's "Prufrock."]

Since the publication of T. S. Eliot's "The Love Song of J. Alfred Prufrock," it is doubtful that any adequately read person has visited an Italian museum without once repeating to himself, "In the room women come and go / Talking of Michelangelo." And it seems probable that E. E. Cummings as well was cognizant of this couplet when he mimicked the "substantial dollarbringing virgins" in his poem "Memorabilia." It may upset Cummings' intentions if we punctuate these stream-on quotations to reveal the trite constructions that they are, but we can then better realize the emptiness of these phrases, which pass between human beings as an excuse for communication: " 'from the Loggia'—'where are we?'—'angels by ...'—'O yes, beautiful'—'we now pass through the'—'look girls!'—'in the style of' " —etc., *ad nauseam*. Cummings presses his point here by means of satire. "Education" is equated with a "thos cook & son" tour. Great art works are nothing more than diversions which allow the dilettante to avoid the "overwhelming question." All the implications of Eliot's couplet are found in this stanza by Cummings also.

The similarity between "Memorabilia" and "Prufrock," however, runs still more deeply, for both poems are essentially wanderings in which the poet invites the reader to accompany him. "stop look & / listen" is certainly indicative of a different voice than "Let us go then you and I," but both introductions are invitations to join a very special expatriot's tour of his new exile post. Eliot leads his reader "through certain half-deserted streets," while Cummings makes his way through the canals of Venice and along the well-strolled bank of the Riva Schiavoni. Prufrock, the more candid of the two, turns inward to expose his impotence, while Cummings reveals the same signs of spiritual emptiness and sexual sterility in the situation which surrounds him. He decries "the coming of the Americans" who have transported themselves across the sea, it seems, solely to corrupt his haven and to harass with him their insensitivity and prudery. But the inference is common to both poems; the escape has not been successful, for the "overwhelming question" remains unasked and unanswered. In exasperation Cummings concludes the poem at once bemoaning and mocking his condition—"(O to be a metope / now that triglyph's here)"—that is, to find a meaningfulness in life which would place him in the universe with the same comfortable precision with which a metope fits between two triglyphs in the Doric order. Yet even here, despite Cummings' humor, there is a surprising congruence with "Prufrock," for the metope is, incidentally, also the middle anterior portion of a crab, the segment from which the pincers extend. "I should have been a pair of ragged claws / Scuttling across the floors of silent seas" is how Eliot painfully said it.

Cummings' "Memorabilia" was published almost a decade after "Prufrock," and in terms of theme, one might charge that Cummings borrowed heavily from Eliot. Yet viewing the intellectual climate of the 'teens and 'twenties, this is not a serious criticism. What is important, rather, is the very individual brand of success which Cummings achieves in his poem—a voice quite distinct from Eliot's. Eliot speaking eruditely is the Prince Hamlet he claims not to be, while it is actually Cummings speaking by means of puns and riddles who is "at times the Fool." Cummings substitutes ingenuity for Eliot's esotericism. When Cummings resorts to Italian to achieve the purposes of his poem, he tells the reader "that means ... ," but the quotation from Dante's *Inferno*, when it prefaces Eliot's poem, remains untranslated for most readers. An image as precise as Eliot's "I have measured out my life with coffee spoons" is none the less reminiscent of Bohemian pastimes. Cummings, however, reworks the popular American idiom—"mine eyes have seen / the glory of"—to bring the message of "Prufrock" into terms of a more common experience.

Cummings' third stanza, beginning with "i do signore," for all its intended confusion, is nevertheless the keystone of the poem. When one clears away the repetitive interjections of "signore" and "gondola," which serve as verbal local color, the lines simply appear descriptive. Yet the attentive reader can patch together from the beginning and ending of this stanza one very revealing statement: "I do affirm that ... God only ... knows ... i don't." Cummings here exhibits the basis for the existential irony which pervades his poem, but, importantly, an irony which, however penetrating, never reaches the extremes of self-flagellation as that of Eliot's.

—H. Seth Finn, "Cummings' 'Memorabilia'," *The Explicator* 29, no. 10 (1971): Item 42.

[In this excerpt from his book on Cummings's poetry, Lane provides some historical and literary context for the poem and discusses the effects of its ironic tone.]

Yeats's words that serve as epigraph to this chapter—they are from his essay "Discoveries"—suggest the basis of Cummings' satire in "MEMORABILIA." "What," the Irishman had asked rhetorically, "is the value of an education ... that does not begin with the personality?" Cummings' poem, portrait of a Venice fragmented, illuminates this lament. The tourists here painted have become acquirers rather than creators, for their education began not with the personality but with that external to it. They have learned to purchase, photograph, and catalogue ideas and objects, but they connect nothing of art and culture with themselves. Failing to sense the inherent contradiction between absorbing the stones of Venice and discussing them in "rancid voices," they destroy the very culture they stalk. On a trip to Venice made the same year as "MEMORABILIA," Cummings saw the "intrinsically wrong ... sign 'SOMETHING NEW, CHEAP AND BEAUTIFUL'" and observed sadly that this "glittering slogan ... reflects, all too well, our own nation's slip-shod method of thought." Money changers, in short—either acquisitive tourists or the predatory hawkers that spring up around them—profane art's temples as well as God's. And where, as in Venice, the two are one, a whole city may grow gaunt amidst the din.

A title, always noteworthy when it occurs in Cummings' work, sets the tone of this poem. Echoing Robert Browning, who died in Venice and whose lines will be modified for the poem's close, it gathers at once both loss and irony. Browning's "Memorabilia" fixes on the remembered moment, the image that remains when its context has vanished:

> I crossed a moor, with a name of its own
> And a certain use in the world no doubt,
> Yet a hand's-breadth of it shines alone
> 'Mid the blank miles round about:

For there I picked upon the heather
And there I put inside my breast
A moulted feather, an eagle-feather!
Well, I forget the rest.

Cummings' Venetian eagle-feather, the image that remains after splendors of history, art, and architecture are forgotten, is this dramatic vocal impression of a city fragmented. In its idiomatic mixture of Browning, railroad talk, Dante, Julia Ward Howe, and the King James Bible, in its contrapuntal treatment of poetic speaker and omnipresent gondolier, and above all in its vocal cacophony of female tourists, the poems recreates a modern Babel.

Yet Venice once ruled the seas. From this city Marco Polo had begun his famous journeys; to it Dante had been sent as ambassador by Guido da Polenta. As late as 1911 Mann's Gustav Aschenbach could think: "Wenn man über Nacht das Unvergleichliche, das mächenhaft Abweichende zu erreichen wünschte, wohin ging man? Aber das war klar." Fifteen years later, though—to a perhaps less tolerant observer—the city was virtually dead, its mysterious balance of East and West overwhelmed by the influx of Americanism. Cummings quotes a gondolier—"Venice, city of silence & poetry, is murdered by motorboats" (*L* 248)—and leaves, at and in the city's wake, this memorabilia.

The precision here is difficult to set down, but it resides in ironies. Once a center of culture, sea power Venice has become accessible primarily by train, has devolved into a mere railroad crossing. Once a home of learned men, Venice is now visited by mistranslation, Dante's "nel mezzo del cammin'"—"in the middle of the journey," the allegorical beginning of the *Divina Commedia*—here misrendered "half- / way up the Campanile," the tower before St. Mark's cathedral. These invaders are not God's forces, the grim waves of Civil War soldiers in Miss Howe's "Battle Hymn of the Republic," but money's, "the substantial dollarbringing virgins." And though Cummings' description of them involves comedies of pun and especially sound—"armed with ... legs," "Baedekers Mothers and kodaks," "in / the felicitous vicinity"—his poem tramples out the vintage of wrath's grapes.

The opening, long sentence of "Memorabilia" establishes the poem's theme and tonality; the remainder consists of two variations on that theme and a coda. First is the almost operatic counterpoint of harassed speaker and persistent gondolier, an uncomfortable duet whose occurrence the speaker blames on money. As the duet develops, sense, straightforward, becomes less important than sound; "gondola" (its accent is on the initial syllable) merges with "Omaha" and "Altoona," and the passage moves toward a comically ridiculous fusion of the United States and Italy. It reaches this in "Cincingondolanati," the unmusical affidavit that buyer and seller are indissolubly and ruinously interdependent. There follows a cinematic passage, rapid cuts jarring against one another until, regardless of conventional content, technique itself makes statement. Within the quotation marks I hear fourteen different (or alternating) voices—all at cross purposes, none identifiable—and the effect of their running together is a dramatic aural metaphor. "Only connect," E. M. Forster prefaced *Howards End*, and we see here the consequences of ignoring him. Amidst the decaying but still appreciable splendors of Venice, John Ruskin and anonymous Marjorie have nothing to say to each other. Faced with magnificent buildings and paintings, the disconnected tourist can feel only with her second-head sensibility, speak only in her trivializing idiom; beneath the awesome shadow of *San Marco*, she asks: "isn't this wellcurb simply darling."

The poem's coda, superb in its crescendo of O's, gathers final scorn. Its juxtaposition of "Education" and "thos cook & son" (purveyors of Cook's tours and once the cheapest traveler's checks) suggests the unholy alliance between knowledge and money that has led to the desecration of Venice and the ruin of her destroyers. The final lines, harkening back to an echo in the title, alter Browning's "Home-Thoughts, from Abroad." "Oh to be in England / Now that April's there," the homesick Englishman had written, but Cummings, longing for a change of atmosphere rather than place, wishes only to be free of the cacophony that precedes this coda. In "O to be a metope / now that triglyph's here," he replaces Browning's poignance with comedy—the chime of "be" and "metope" is as responsible for this difference as the shift in language—and offers an ironic summary of his feelings. Desiring to be a metope, the space in a

Doric frieze between projecting, ornamental triglyphs, Cummings would disappear from the loud and aggressive young women of his land. Casting a last, parenthesized Venetian stone, the poet exits with a stage whisper, trailing his dismay at the "marriageable nymph" abroad.

—Gary Lane, *I Am: A Study of E. E. Cummings' Poems* (Lawrence: The University Press of Kansas, 1976): 81–85.

"i sing of Olaf glad and big"

Two of the most common criticisms leveled at Cummings are that his body of work displays little development over time and that the humans inhabiting his poems are shallow and immature. Both claims are refuted by "i sing of Olaf glad and big" (*ViVa*, 1931), an abridged but powerful epic for the modern era in which Cummings, five years after skewering easy-target tourists in "Memorabilia," wields the same razor-sharp wit and biting satire to champion an entirely new kind of war hero.

The opening stanza fires a volley straight into the face of tradition. While parodying the opening lines of Virgil's *Aeneid* ("I sing of arms and a man") the narrator introduces *his* hero as a man famous not for feats of stupendous bloodshed but for his conscientious objection. Typical of Cummings' witticisms, the forced rhyme of "war" and "object-or" accomplishes two things at once: first, it parodies the strained translations of classical epics that Cummings was no doubt forced to read at Harvard, and second, by separating out the word "object" it emphasizes the inhuman treatment Olaf receives for his beliefs. This opening stanza, then, as in many of Cummings's works, contains a kind of schematic for how to read the rest of the poem, warning the reader to be on the lookout for other inversions, puns, allusions, and sarcasm.

The next stanza describes the first of several sadistic ordeals to which Cummings's hero is subjected. Escorted by a West Point-educated colonel, Olaf is sent through a hazing gauntlet of "noncoms" (noncommissioned officers) who "knock" him on the head, freeze him with ice water, scour him with "muddy" toilet brushes and strike him with various "blunt instruments." All that is clear enough, but other words and phrases in the stanza benefit from further elucidation. "Wellbeloved," "most succinctly bred," and "kindred intellects" are obviously used satirically to question what kind of men, and by extension what kind of society, would sanction such brutality. The dictionary gives two definitions for "trig," a word of Scandinavian origin meaning "pleasingly neat, trim, or orderly" and "loyal"—characteristics commonly associated with good soldiers. "Olaf" is also Scandinavian, however, and loyal to his own ideals, so "trig" could carry ironic connotations as well. Specifying the colonel's West Point pedigree holds the entire military leadership responsible for the aping actions of the enlisted men, here dubbed "noncoms" in a winking nod to both military slang and Cummings's own habit of adding prefixes to common words to create neologistic antonyms (e.g., "unworld," "nonsun," etc.).

Despite being stripped naked ("wanting any rag / upon what God unto him gave") and beaten half to death ("being to all intents a corpse"), Olaf calmly refuses to kowtow. That he does not fight back, that he "responds without getting annoyed," is critical to Cummings's message. For Olaf's heroism lies not in action, but in his unwillingness to subjugate his personal ethics to those of the mindless majority. He is not a grandstanding rebel with a cause, but a true pacifist. In this way, he is more closely akin to Melville's "Bartleby" than fellow conscientious objector Mohammed Ali. Nevertheless, his own brand of nobility is asserted by the use of a capital "I"—an honor that Cummings does not extend to his narrator.

It may be difficult, given its contemporary currency, for today's readers to perceive the visceral impact of the word "Fuck" that Cummings drops at the end of this stanza, but needless to say, at the time the poem was published (three years before Joyce's *Ulysses* won its obscenity trial and beat back the censors), anyone of delicate sensibilities not already inflamed by Cummings' anti-hero would have been standing at full attention. Using the expletive in a treasonous statement only heightens the effect. But Cummings is not merely trying to shock his readers here. He is also hoping to raise the question of which is the greater evil: foul-mouthed, conscientious objection or officially approved torture?

The next couplet provides a little comic relief from the sadism, depicting the colonel in a cartoonish doubletake. Doubtless he is reacting as much to Olaf's "oath" as to his stubborn resolve. The adjective "silver" conjures both a medal-bedecked uniform and a graying head of hair, both symbols of the old world order that the narrator is trying to unseat. In the face of anomalous, individualistic behavior, the colonel can only think to go shave. This reaction betrays his overly-regimented brain and provides a few more laughs, until the reader realizes that his absence will allow the savagery to continue unsupervised.

Sure enough, the torment continues in the next stanza, with "blueeyed" officers and "firstclassprivates" cursing, kicking, and ultimately sodomizing Olaf with red hot bayonets. As Olaf's treatment gets more puerile, so do the narrator's puns. The use of "rectum" and "shit" not only resumes the shock treatment; it also helps uncover the insult in "firstclassprivates." After all the kicking and screaming, it is the soldiers' "voices and boots" that are "much the worse" for the wear. Olaf just continues to repeat himself.

In the following stanza, Cummings carries his indictment all the way up to the Commander-in-chief, who toes the line like everybody else and throws Olaf in prison, "where he died." Next to come under fire is Christ himself, whose "mercy infinite" apparently does not extend to fellow pacifists.

After taking thrusts at the entire military, the President, and the Savior, the narrator cannot help but swing his weapon in one last, wide arc that encompasses both himself and the reader. None of us are free of guilt, he suggests, if we stand by and let this kind of thing happen. And what is worse, none of us is safe. If a big, "blond" (i.e., all-American), and truly brave individual can get snuffed out by mob rule for holding a contrary opinion, then what is to prevent any of us from suffering the same fate?

CRITICAL VIEWS ON
"i sing of Olaf glad and big"

ROBERT E. WEGNER ON DEPTH OF CHARACTERIZATION

[Robert E. Wegner has taught English at Alma College
and was also co-editor of *The Third Coast: Contemporary
Michigan Fiction*. He has published stories and reviews in
Carleton, *Miscellany*, *American Literature*, and *Literary
Review*. In this selection from his book on Cummings,
Wegner uses "i sing of Olaf" to refute the claim that
characters in Cummings's poems are shallowly-rendered
caricatures.]

From an early poetry of exuberance and sensory detail in which
values were seldom pointedly stated, Cummings moved during
the mid-twenties to a position from which he more
pronouncedly rejects the sham values and superficial by-products
of social convention. However, the charge that in his middle and
later poetry he became so obsessed with his own integrity as an
individual that he could neither accept nor find place for the
opinions of others is without warrant in the light of the many
poems he has written for the express purpose of giving credit and
extending praise to those he admired. Equally unwarranted is the
assertion that the characters of his poems are so shallowly
depicted as to emerge almost entirely as caricatures, intensely
presented in objective detail but lacking in substance of thought
or feeling. Numerous poems and prose comments indicate the
opposite, among them those lauding Hart Crane, Ezra Pound,
Froissart, Ford Madox Ford, Picasso, Sally Rand, Jimmy Savo,
Sam (whose "heart was big / as the world aint square)," his father,
and Olaf, "a conscientious object-or," to name those that come
most readily to mind.

The last mentioned poem, "i sing of Olaf glad and big," from
W (*ViVa*), is worth examining, for it depicts a character in terms
other than caricature, does not depend upon objective detail
alone, and demonstrates that thought and feeling are not alien to
the poet's heroes.

Although it is difficult to determine just what a critic may be

49

demanding by the terms "thinking" and "feeling" as attributes of character, it is possible to ascribe to Olaf conscious opinion and certain easily recognized emotions. For example, Olaf upholds his opinion about war not through overt retaliation of insult for insult, not through petty schemes of personal revenge—courses obviously not open to him, since in rejecting war he is rejecting cruelty and sadism—but through a patient acceptance of abuse. However, as evidenced in the two remarks ascribed to him, he does not willingly endure the suffering and torture inflicted upon him. He does not conceive of himself as a martyr dying for some cause; he simply has no use for war. Unlike his persecutors, he will not succumb to playing the role of a caricature; he will not allow himself to be typed as one of those regimented for the express purpose of inflicting misery and perhaps death upon others. Olaf's concept of patriotism and loyalty differs from that of the "nation's blueeyed pride," for it has nothing to do with organized killing. Because he will not conform, because he upholds a belief widely accepted as not practical, he emerges as an individual. The role he plays, though patient, is not passive; he retorts from his position of ignoble humility with the only weapon at his disposal—brutal invective couched in terms his tormentors understand. Because Olaf reveres the dignity of the human being, he has pride. Because he cannot help but react when this dignity is denied or rejected, he is capable of anger. Finally, as Cummings pointedly indicates, Olaf has that rare caliber of courage which compels him to die not for a cause but because of a cause, not for his country but because of his country.

—Robert E. Wegner, *The Poetry and Prose of E. E. Cummings*, (New York: Harcourt, Brace & World, 1965): 99–101.

BETHANY K. DUMAS ON THE USE OF TRADITIONAL METER

[Bethany K. Dumas is Associate Professor of English and Chair of the Linguistics Program at the University of Texas. She has written extensively on linguistics and edits the electronic newsletter *Language in the Judicial Process*. In this excerpt from her book on Cummings, Dumas identifies the meter of the poem and asserts that

Cummings used metrical verse for his more "serious" work.]

Those who think of Cummings as the poet of lowercase letters, scrambled words, and largely unpronounceable poems are always surprised to learn how many and what excellent poems he wrote rising traditional metrical features. Really, the most interesting— and often the most successful—of his poems are those which are nonce forms using traditional metrical patterns. They become most important after *is 5*, which begins a turning point in Cummings' poetic development. As Norman Friedman has pointed out, it is by that volume becoming apparent that in general Cummings reserves metrical stanzas for his more "serious" poems, while he uses experiments for various kinds of free verse embodiments of satire, comedy, and description. The "serious" poems are not all solemn. They are serious in that they embody a more complex view of the universe—and man's place in it—than is possible in the other poems. It is in these that Cummings' transcendent vision is more thoroughly revealed and in which love is described in terms of a transcendental metaphor. Satire is also included; one early example is a satiric poem on the subject of war. First published in *W [ViVa]* (1931), it involves the story of Olaf, a conscientious objector modeled on someone Cummings had met at Camp Devens. In the poem Olaf is first hazed, then tortured, and finally put to death because he does not believe in war. The poem consists of forty-two lines, the pattern for each of which is an eight-syllable, four-stress line, with occasional three-stress lines for variation. The basic foot is the iamb; the basic metrical pattern, iambic tetrameter, is one traditionally used for satiric purposes. While no overall rhyme scheme divides the poem into regular stanzas, there is a discernible impulse toward order; lines are interlocked, and motifs are picked up by the rhyme, even though it is not regular. In that respect it is similar to the three long poems of *Tulips and Chimneys*, particularly "Puella Mea." From its opening lines—"i sing of Olaf glad and big / whose warmest heart recoiled at war:"—to its inevitable conclusion, it is a poem dominated by suggestions of scatology and emphasis upon the discrepancies of which institutional life is always compounded. Olaf speaks twice, once to announce that he "will not kiss your f.ing flag," once to re-affirm "there is some s. I will not eat." Olaf ends in a dungeon; the poem concludes on this note:

> Christ(of His mercy infinite)
> pray to see; and Olaf, too
>
> preponderatingly because
> unless statistics lie he was
> more brave than me:more blond than you.
> (I, 339)

The more serious of the satiric poems always contain a sense of moral indignation, sometimes moral outrage. Like other satirists, Cummings sometimes makes use of scatology and the so-called four-letter Anglo-Saxon words to communicate his outrage. Here the outrage is directed at war, generally; more specifically, though, it is not war that is such hell, but the people who play at war games: the officers, products of socalled military schools; the noncommissioned officers; the enlisted men: and, above all, their commander-in-chief, the President of the United States. Nor is society spared; it is suggested in the closing lines that Olaf, whose name tells the reader that he was probably either foreign-born or a first-generation American, was braver than many citizens doing what they considered their duty, and blonder (i.e., purer) than other Americans. The appeal to statistics is somewhat ironic, for Cummings normally had no use for them.

Olaf is an early type of the individual in Cummings' poems. While "mostpeople" are content to do their duty, even a duty carried out when the laws and conventions are suspended, individuals perform the most heroic of tasks: they remain themselves.

—Bethany K. Dumas, *E. E. Cummings: A Remembrance of Miracles*, (New York, Barnes & Noble, 1974): 84–85

GARY LANE ON THE REVERSAL OF CLASSICAL EXPECTATION

[In this extract from his study of Cummings's poetry, Lane contends that the poem retains its power despite its ironic tone.]

"Arma virumque" sang Vergil, beginning an epic distinguished for its civility; Cummings, adopting and adapting that classical form, sings the man alone. The difference is implicative of both the spirit and the art of Cummings' poem. Olaf embraces an integrity of private rather than public convictions; acknowledging only his personal sense of truth rather than merging his will with the gods', he is a veritable anti-Aeneas, a new kind of hero. His poem, "i sing of Olaf glad and big," neatly reverses classical expectation by a series of ironic twists. It is a small new epic, but one that accumulates considerable power despite its formal miniature.

From the outset, the poem's force resides primarily in its play upon heroic tradition. We learn not "the anger of Peleus' son Achilleus / and its destruction" (Lattimore's translation), but the gentleness of Olaf, "whose warmest heart recoiled at war"; big and blond, our hero may be the physical image of the Germanic warrior, but his temperament is otherwise. The form does not undercut heroism—we do not deal here with mock epic—it instead offers alternative heroic values. In the *Iliad*, Achilles is a hero of physical strength, sulking like a child when Briseis is taken from him, but at last achieving immortality by slaughtering Trojans. Olaf's strength is moral. Scarcely annoyed as his self-righteous and sadistic torturers attempt to strip him of human dignity, he achieves epic stature by *refusing* to kill.

The shift has important implications. Heroic epic, from the *Iliad* to the *Chanson de Roland*, is based on communal values; a hero's greatness is a measure of the degree to which he exemplifies the qualities his society most prizes. With Olaf it is different. He must give up not merely his life but also the good name that valiance customarily wins, the hero's renown and reputation, υλέος. He can do so lightly, however, defying both the military force of his nation and its massively conformed opinions, because he answers to an individual rather than a collective truth, to personal vision rather than social regard.

Cummings' instrument of truth here is irony. From the beginning of the poem to the underplayed tribute of its final lines, we are led to ponder the relationship between what things seem and what they are. Thus, "recoiled," suggesting not the jump of a fired gun but the heart's horrified reaction to it, offers an initial perspective on the matter of war, flicks the first stone at traditional heroic glory. As the irony gathers, Cummings unmasks the modern bankruptcy of collective values. In a society so perverted that torture has become socially correct—it is administered by the "wellbelovéd colonel (trig / westpointer most succinctly bred)"—sometimes only profanity can express the sacred heart. Refusing to "kiss your fucking flag," Olaf avoids the polite Latin that in our century has time and again been used to justify atrocity. His taut Anglo-Saxon, direct as his behavior, is comment enough on his suave persecutors.

The ironies of the poem, then, sadly fulfill the implication of its early wordplay: conscientiously nonviolent Olaf has indeed become an "object" to the soulless torturers that surround him. In response to his love—the essence of nonviolence—he is beaten; in the face of his courage, "our president" finds him a "yellowsonofabitch." Yet the poem has greater impact than the customary moral fable. Cummings' laconic conclusion—a touch of Auden that Auden himself would use a few years later in "The Unknown Citizen"—forces us to deeper involvement than the approving nod. Its unusual comparison of hero with poet and reader—"unless statistics lie he was / more brave than me: more blond than you"—suddenly strips away the comfortable distance that a morally simple struggle has erected for us. The speaker's irony in adopting the yardstick of Olaf's murderers, his invocation not of the muse—the visionary heart's truth—but of statistics, democracy's lowest common denominator, compels us to attend the casual equation of blondness and bravery, requires us not only to distinguish but to choose between appearance and reality; and the poem's stark duality leaves no room for middling heroics. Thus at the close we are denied the aristocratic pleasure of being an audience to epic, are instead thrown into the simple dramatic world of the form itself. We cannot reflectively sit in judgment, but are moved to ask uncomfortable—and perhaps life-giving—questions about ourselves.

—Gary Lane, *I Am: A Study of E. E. Cummings' Poems*, (Lawrence, Kansas: UP of Kansas, 1976): 39–41.

MICHAEL J. COLLINS ON FORMAL ALLUSION

[Michael J. Collins is a Professor of English and Dean of the School for Summer and Continuing Education at

Although we might guess Eliot, it was Robert Frost who said that "a poem is best read in the light of all the other poems ever written.... Progress is not the aim, but circulation."[1] What Frost is expressing here, of course, is a characteristically modern recognition of the relationship between a particular poem and what Eliot calls "the existing order,"[2] a recognition that, among other things, leads readers and writers of modern poetry to see allusion as an important and useful poetic device. Yet in spite of our modern concern with tradition and the accompanying sensitivity to allusion, as readers of modern poetry we frequently overlook or undervalue the type of allusion that might be called "formal allusion." What follows here then is an attempt to suggest the importance and the frequency of this type of allusion in modern poetry—to show, inductively, that form in modern poetry is often allusive and functions to remind us of other poems written in the same form and thus to create a context in which we are to read the poem at hand.[3] (...)

One other poem that should be discussed in the context of formal allusion is "i sing of Olaf glad and big" by E. E. Cummings. In the opening lines of the poem,

> I sing of Olaf glad and big
> whose warmest heart recoiled at war:
> a conscientious object-or,[12]

the "I sing of Olaf" alludes, of course, to the epic tradition in general, while the humorous forced rhyme of "war" and "object-or" alludes particularly to the translations by Dryden and Pope of classical epic into English heroic couplets. Once we recognize in the forced rhyme that Cummings is alluding to these translations and that his quick, bouncing, and sometimes comic tetrameter lines are to be heard in contrast to such longer, slower, dignified, and stately pentameter lines as

> Arms, and the Man I sing, who, forc'd by Fate,
> And haughty *Juno's* unrelenting Hate;

Expell'd and exil'd, left the *Trojan* Shoar:
Long Labours, both by Sea and Land he bore,[13]

once we begin to read "I sing of Olaf" in the context of, say,
Dryden's translation of the *Aeneis*, we realize that Cummings is
pretending to work in a new genre, not the mock-epic, but what
we might call the modern epic or, more exactly, the "upside down
epic."

In addition to the forced rhyme and the contrasting
tetrameter lines, other devices in the poem remind us in one way
or another of Dryden's translation. The lines

> but—though an host of overjoyed
> noncoms (first knocking on the head
> him) do through icy waters roll
> that helplessness which others stroke,

with their syntactic involution suggest such characteristic
involutions in Dryden as

> A second Spear, which kept the former Course,
> From the same Hand, and sent with equal Force,
> His right Arm pierc'd, and holding on, bereft
> His use of both and pinion'd down his left (p. 1332).

The officialese of "our president, being of which / assertions duly
notified" and the simple, straight forward, colloquial vulgarity of
Olaf's heroic understatement "'there is some s. I will not eat'"
contrast with the long, formal, dignified speeches of traditional
epic heroes. And here, of course, is the reason for the form, the
reason for writing an upside down epic that is the opposite in
form and manner of Dryden and Pope's renditions of the classical
epics. Olaf is a modern epic hero, but his heroism, unlike that of
the warriors of old, lies in his refusal to fight and thus since he is,
as it were, the contradiction of the conventional epic hero, his
poem must be a contradiction of the familiar epic form. From this
point of view then, it is clear that the poem is not to be taken as a
mock epic, for while we may find the short, bouncing, involuted
lines, the unexpected rhymes, the sudden shifts in diction, and the
satirical asides humorous, we are asked finally to admire Olaf and
to take his heroism and the form that reveals it seriously.

NOTES

1. "The Prerequisites," in *Selected Prose of Robert Frost*, ed. Hyde Cox and Edward Connery Lathem (New York: Holt, Rinehart and Winston, 1966), p. 97.

2. "Tradition and the Individual Talent," in *Selected Essays*, new ed. (New York: Harcourt, Brace and Company, 1950), p. 5. In her book called *Robert Frost on Writing* (New Brunswick, N.J.: Rutgers Univ. Press, 1973) Elaine Barry points out that Frost's "Views ... of the artist's interaction with the past" are similar to those of Eliot (p. 3) and then goes on to cite as evidence the two passages from "The Prerequisites" and "Tradition and the Individual Talent" (pp. 3–4).

3. Form, of course, is a tricky word, and I am using it here to refer only to meter, rhythm, rhyme, and stanzaic pattern and to such familiar fixed forms as the heroic couplet, the sonnet, and the ballad stanza. I should also point out that although what I am calling formal allusion seems close to the types of allusion the *Princeton Encyclopedia of Poetry and Poetics* call "imitative allusion" and "structural allusion," neither term quite describes what I have in mind, for as defined by E[arl] M[iner] in the *Encyclopedia*, "imitative allusion" seems to include more than just form, at least as I am using the word, and "structural allusion" seems to refer to the overall coherence and logical progression of a work of art. See "Allusion" in *Princeton Encyclopedia of Poetry and Poetics*, ed. Alex Preminger (Princeton: Princeton Univ. Press, 1965).

12. All citations of "i sing of Olaf glad and big" are from E. E. Cummings, *Poems 1923–1954* (New York: Harcourt, Brace and World, 1954), pp. 244–5.

13. John Dryden, trans., "Virgil's Aeneis," in *The Poems of John Dryden*, ed. James Kinsley (Oxford: Clarendon Press, 1958), III, 1064. All citations of the work are from this edition and will be given in the text.

—Michael J. Collins, "Formal Allusion in Modern Poetry," *Concerning Poetry* 9, no. 1 (1976): 5, 8–9, 10-11.

RUSHWORTH M. KIDDER ON THE EFFECT OF INCONGRUITIES IN TONE

[Rushworth M. Kidder is founder and president of the Institute for Global Ethics. He is a journalist, interviewer, and commentator and the author of *How Good People Make Tough Choices: Resolving the Dilemma of Ethical Living* and several other books. In this selection from his book on Cummings, Kidder examines the aesthetic results of the poem's abrupt shifts in tone and diction.]

Adopting carefully metrical rhythm and perfect rhyme as he often did for explicit and unambiguous satires, [Cummings] tells with great narrative economy the story of Olaf, the "conscientious object-or" who was treated, as the latter word implies, less as person than object. The tale is a grim one of vengeance and torture inflicted on a draftee whose "heart recoiled at war." Yet the tone is everywhere light, an effect achieved less by the narrative presentation of incongruities—a common enough device in humorous writing—than by the use of poetic techniques that create a sense of parody. Imitating the grand style of Virgil, the poet begins not with "I sing of arms and the man" but with "i sing of Olaf." The relentless rhyme scheme and tetrameter pattern lend a singsong effect, driving the poem gaily forward no matter what the words are saying. The words themselves are incongruously drawn from various sources. Using his typical blend of stuffy formality ("our president, being of which / assertions duly notified"), colloquialism ("the yellowsonofabitch"), obscenity ("your fucking flag"), and archaisms ("anent"), Cummings also mixes straightforward word order with the most ludicrous rearrangements designed to bring a word into rhyming position. These, along with a generous sprinkling of clichés ("nation's blueeyed pride"), redundancies ("bayonets roasted hot with heat"), and echoes of an earlier poetic language ("Christ(of His mercy infinite / i pray to see; and Olaf, too"), combine to create a poem whose delight is not in untangling the ambiguities but in riding the abrupt shifts of diction and surprising conjunctions of tone, and whose skillfulness is revealed in descriptions of singular aptness ("trig / westpointer most succinctly bred") which draw the most unexpected words into effective relationships. Not unlike Picasso's *Three Musicians* (1921), which as Alfred Barr noted is a happy subject full of bright colors that nevertheless produces a most somber tone, Cummings' poem makes of the most somber subject a poem which, true to the satirist's art, has about it an astringent humor.

—Rushworth M. Kidder, *E.E. Cummings: An Introduction to the Poetry*, (New York: Columbia University Press, 1979): 92–93.

"somewhere i have never traveled, gladly beyond"

The poems discussed so far have shown a Cummings steeped in classical and medieval influences, a scornful satirist, skillful punster, and staunch defender of the nonconformist. What we have not seen is the transcendental Cummings, a mode he began to adopt more frequently as he aged and one that, most commentators agree, represents the apex of his artistic development and the most mature expression of his personal philosophy. For a good summation of this philosophy we again turn to Cummings himself, and the last of his "nonlectures":

> "I am someone who proudly and humbly affirms that love is the mystery-of-mysteries and that nothing measurable matters 'a very good God damn': that 'an artist, a man, a failure' is no mere ... automaton, but a naturally and miraculously whole human being ... whose only happiness is to transcend himself, whose every agony is to grow."

These beliefs place Cummings in the tradition of other Transcendentalists, from Emerson onward, who contend that ultimate truths cannot be quantified or proved, but only perceived directly by the imagination and/or intuition. To write poetry about things like love, death, and the meaning of life, then, he had to find a means to recreate the moment of epiphany that lays such mysteries bare—in other words, to somehow express that which is, by its very definition, ineffable. Throughout the course of his career, Cummings came up with an amazing array of techniques for doing this—from profoundly simple examples of Nature at work to complex experiments in typography, syntax, and grammar that transformed the English language itself. Many of these innovations lie outside the scope of this volume, but "somewhere i have never travelled" (*ViVa*, 1931) provides an excellent introduction to how Cummings the transcendentalist approaches the "mystery-of-mysteries."

Love's intangibility is the subject of the opening stanza. Love, at least as he is currently experiencing it, is not a place the narrator has ever "travelled" to before, nor is it something he can "touch." The phrase "your eyes have their silence" in the second line provides more evidence that his five standard senses have failed him. Synaesthesia, or a co-mingling of two or more senses, is a common technique in poetry to convey derangement or extreme intensity. Here, Cummings uses it to hint at something beyond the narrator's understanding, something simultaneously unseen and unspoken. And yet it is precisely these ethereal "things" contained in his lover's "most frail gesture" that give the narrator a comforting sense of enclosure.

The metaphors get a little more concrete in the next stanza, but they are by no means commonplace. Instead of the traditional comparing of the beloved to a flower—e.g. "*O my luve's like a red, red rose*" (Robert Burns)—the narrator likens *himself* to a rose and his lover to the "Spring" that brings him to bloom. By inverting the roles, Cummings not only reinvigorates the old trope, he also expands its connotations to include the bittersweet mixture of elation and vulnerability that love effects. He is powerless to resist, despite the past heartbreak and bitterness implied by the line "though i have closed myself as fingers." The sense of a seasonal, cyclic rebirth is reinforced by the multiple openings and closings within this one stanza, as well as the poem's movement from "Spring" to "snow" to "rain."

His lover's dominion is enlarged in the next stanza to include the power to close, as well as to open. When compared to the neutral sound of "close," "shut" is a jolting, almost onomatopoetic evocation of the narrator being walled off from the rest of world. Juxtaposing "shut" with the adverb "beautifully" suggests the narrator accepts her power and finds beauty in the act of entrusting his life to her. The second adverb, "suddenly," harkens back to the first line of "let's live suddenly without thinking" (*Tulips & Chimneys*), another Cummings poem in which Nature's blueprint for how to be truly alive is transmitted via subconscious, non-logical connections—a concept further developed by the use of "heart" and "imagines" in the next line of "somewhere i have never travelled." Instead of perceiving the snow through some sensory appendage or genetic predisposition, the flower uses its heart and its imagination. If we somehow miss the transcendental implications of this, the narrator drives them home in the opening lines of the fourth stanza. "The power of your intense fragility" also employs a paradoxical pairing of opposites to convey how transcendental qualities defy conventional language, just as they defy conventional means of "perceiving" them. In the next critical analysis we will discuss how Cummings uses this technique to even greater effect in "my father moved through dooms of love."

Cummings again uses synaesthesia in the last two lines of the fourth stanza, together with a whole bevy of transcendental metaphors that add infinite complexity to what is being described. "Texture" and "colour" are conflated to evoke a kind of living relief map, complete with multiple "countries" and capable, "with each breathing," of "rendering death" powerless and "forever" possible. Cummings realizes he has waded into some deep waters here that threaten to drown both his subject and the reader in abstraction, so he pulls back in the last stanza and admits that they're all just metaphors, and inadequate ones at that. Ultimately, he may never be able to say exactly "what it is about [her] that closes and opens." "Not even the rain" will provide him with an apt metaphor for conveying the life-giving power of her tiny hands. And yet, somehow, the silence in her eyes has been transformed into a voice that "something in [him] understands" and that makes all the difference. By working through the metaphors and attempting to imagine for himself what love is and what it means, by accepting that love is a never-ending process of "opening" and "closing," he has achieved a transcendental understanding, reflected in the perfect rhyme of the last four lines.

"somewhere i have never traveled, gladly beyond"

Rushworth M. Kidder on Paradox and the Appearance of Simplicity

[In this excerpt, Kidder identifies the many uses of paradox in the poem, revealing the complexity of expression hiding beneath the surface.]

The sequence [in *ViVa*] which comprises poems in praise of love and lovers (poems LVII–LXIII) opens with the justly famous "somewhere i have never travelled, gladly beyond" (LVII). A complex piece, it depends on an appearance of simplicity. Using commonplace diction ("intense" and "fragility" are perhaps the only words an elementary-schooler might pause over), Cummings builds the poem largely out of monosyllabic words either by themselves or attached to ordinary suffixes. The subject, too, is uncomplicated: images of eyes and hands interweave their themes of opening, closing, and touching. Rhythmically, the poem is probably best construed as free verse lines gathered into stanzas, although a case can be made for sprung rhythm pentameter. The last stanza locks into perfect rhyme; previous stanzas conform to no rhyme scheme, although occasional hints ("enclose me" / "unclose me"; "descending" / "breathing"; and the anticipatory "and" and "rose") prepare for the last stanza's rhymes on the significant words "closes" and "hands."

Part of the poem's success lies in its skillful assimilation of complexity into an easily apprehended structure. Not unlike the poetry of the Psalms, it has both the initial appeal and the lasting resonance of carefully crafted workmanship. It is built, in fact, on many kinds of subtle paradox. The first two lines seem simple enough: your eyes, says the poet, have a depth to them far beyond any experiencing, an inexhaustible (and so "gladly" constant and trustworthy) inner stillness which is beyond reach. But in context (especially given the "voice of your eyes" in the penultimate line), the "silence" takes on a new and less positive meaning: the unpleasant possibility of a loss of that "voice" is gladly so remote as to be beyond "any experience." Seemingly contradictory, the two meanings here are resolved by providing two meanings for the key word. If "silence" means muffled suppression, the lines deny its power; if it means quiet peace, they affirm its value.

Another sort of paradox appears in the third and fourth lines:

> in your most frail gesture are things which enclose me,
> or which i cannot touch because they are too near.

One has only to work with tools in a tightly cramped space, or to try to touch one's elbow with the fingers on the same hand, to know that nearness and untouchability are compatible attributes. Cummings also planted in "touch" the less physical meaning of *comprehend* or *come to grips with*: your very nearness, the narrator says, shows me how much I am missing.

Punctuation provides paradox in the next stanza. Its second line functions so smoothly as an extension of the first, and so well as an introductory clause for the next lines, that the reader tends to move right through the stanza without pausing to determine where the full stop should fall. The paradox is that our sense of grammar insists on punctuation, while our sense of semantic continuity ignores such restraints.

The paradox of the third stanza is that an inanimate object can be endowed with foresight. The flower, says the poet, need not wait until it *feels* the snow; because it can imagine the future, it closes up in anticipation of bad weather. The fourth stanza hangs its paradox on the standard technique of oxymoron: "the power of your intense fragility" combines strangely dissimilar ideas into an effective characterization of a rose. The lines continue by fusing the usually distinct effects of "texture" and "colour." The last line—"rendering death and forever with each breathing"—takes a universal symbol of life (breath) as a source of death. But it does more: "death and forever" suggests an eternity beyond mere physical dissolution; and "rendering," among its many meanings, means to melt oil out of something, or (in this case, figuratively) to break down and annihilate the structure and substantiality of "death and forever" by the presence of life.

The final stanza admits (as Cummings' poems often admit) to

ignorance: "(i do not know what it is about you that closes / and opens," The poet does understand, however, that a comparison between "all roses" and "the voice of your eyes" proves the supremacy of the latter. The last line ("nobody, not even the rain, has such small hands") summarizes in the word "rain" his ideas of fragility and frailty blended with efficacy and life-giving force.

It is worth noting what is missing here. Like the earlier poem for his mother, there is no trace of irony: the praise is unabashed, unmitigated. Like the more satiric and witty early poems, there is an appearance of formal patterning in the layout of the lines on the page; but unlike them, there is no tight adherence to rhyme and rhythm. Neither is there any attempt at profound philosophic insight. Yet the very simplicity of the idea—that you have the power to control me just as naturally as the weather controls the flowers, and that ultimately you are even more effective than nature—is knitted into a tight web of theme and variation, of progression from images of spring through winter and on into spring again, and of depths that reveal themselves as individual words are plumbed.

—Rushworth M. Kidder, *E. E. Cummings: An Introduction to the Poetry*, (New York: Columbia University Press, 1979): 98–101.

DAVID V. FORREST ON THE LIMITS OF HUMAN EXPERIENCE

[David V. Forrest is a founding member of the E. E. Cummings Society, and chief editor of its journal, *SPRING*. A psychiatrist by profession, he has published several articles on Cummings from a psychoanalytical perspective. In this excerpt from a much longer article, Forrest examines how Cummings employs "poetic defensive processes" to address death and other weighty matters.]

Those of us who were attracted to the poetry of psychoanalysis and not to its oversupply of prose are not likely to be satisfied, as we seek poetry, with verse that is shallow in tone or shy of depths. In my own case, I began to read Cummings as I entered college, soon after first reading Freud. In each the sudden expansion of the verbal domain was surprising, as though one had fallen through a floor of words to an unconsidered level of ideas shining in dark halls and enormous rooms of language. I wrote a thesis on the poet, who was generous in helping me with it. Part of his initial good will seemed to be because I would study medicine in a year and he felt I would not be exploitative. (...)

Cummings has remained my favorite poet; his worn books have never been displaced on my shelves and his paintings hang in my home and my office (after his death I received two paintings of Mt. Chocorua viewed from his New Hampshire Joy Farm, and his wife Marion left me a portrait of herself by Cummings). I would not attempt a dispassionate critical analysis of his work, leaving that to others, of whom there have been many, perhaps none so distinguished as my erstwhile mentor at Princeton, R. P. Blackmur. (...)

I shall also all but eschew biography in my approach here to Cummings' poems, as I still feel unable or uncomfortable in correlating the deeper psychological dimensions I wish to discuss with the life of the poet who had befriended me as a young student.

Let me proceed, before I talk myself out of this enterprise entirely, to the question of whether there might be certain human matters that, in being treated by a poet, might especially elicit the most deeply-lying defenses, those earliest in origin, and those most capable of working at the limits of human experience. I would suggest that a poet of depth might reach to such limits with his language in the exploratory spirit of limit-striving that is characteristic of healthy organisms. Such limits as we may reach do not make for a long list: they are loving, to the limits of passion and orgasm; death; and madness. (...)

Cummings not only addresses these limits (and few poets do), he addresses them in a familiar way that is so easy to approach that the courage that it took may not be noticed. Cummings always dances, as they say in the ballet company, "full out on point." In another sense, Cummings is able to bring these extremes of human experience into his poetry because of the unusual development of what I shall call his poetic defensive processes (to avoid ad hominem referents). (...)

As part of his war with words (to borrow a phrase out of context from Harley Shands), Cummings exploits poetic license in the extreme. Where other poets permitted themselves certain formal and conventional rearrangements of word order, Cummings spectacularly invents *syntactic play* and employs words in unaccustomed ways as parts of speech they have never been before. The result is Cummings' unprecedented contribution to the pursuit of depth in poetry. As we read him we are thrown perforce upon those deeper syntactic structures described by Chomsky to mine the secret ore of meaning that lies beneath reason and words:

> Life is more true than reason will deceive
> (more secret or than madness did reveal)
>
> [*Ps.*, p. 421]

He gives us syntax *lessons* that are needed if we are to hear through (as well as see through) the layers of human intentionality. The use of such an ability has been demonstrated recently in a salutary paper by Dahl et al. (1978) deciphering countertransference messages by clues in syntactic aberrations. This is plainly another level of sophistication in the making of poetry in English that is wholly original in Cummings.[2] (...)

Toward the end of his last book Cummings gives us a poem of deadly mood, of acceptance of coming death and its awesome, other silence (other than the silences of deeply living moments, to which we shall return). It begins with the entry of this silence and contrasts it with the living silences of "singing" flesh:

> enter no (silence is the blood whose flesh
> is singing) silence:but unsinging. In
> spectral such hugest how hush,one
> dead leaf stirring makes a crash

I shall depart, probably unwisely, from my self-imposed rule of biographical silence to say that I had heard from Marion that

Cummings died suddenly and unexpectedly following a massive cerebrovascular accident. I take this poem as representative of Cummings' empathic imagination and foresight rather than as the product of the impact of illness. Its finality make it one of the saddest and most frightening of poems; its feeling lies far too deep for tears. "No silence" but a spectral hush is a terrible deprivation for a poet devoted to the full depth of undistracted sexual passion, of which silence is his regularly stated precondition (the voice, especially of anger, then dismissed). The flesh is not singing; it is sadly unsinging. A spectre in a spectral hush, a dead leaf stirring and waiting to die, he tells the pain of this purposeless existence, that seems so far from the singing flesh of youth.

> —far away(as far as alive) lies
> april;and i breathe-move-and-seem some
> perpetually roaming whylessness—
>
> autumn has gone:will winter never come?

Then the poem shifts. The passivity of waiting is replaced by activity, an exhortation to death as a natural winter:

> o come,terrible anonymity;enfold
> phantom me with the murdering minus of cold
> —open this ghost with millionary knives of wind—

Anonymity is indeed a terrible word for a poet of "who," of the person as individual apart from the anonymous mass of "mostpeople." Already phantom, a ghost of himself he awaits "opening." The sadness of this opening is that it is not an expansion of the self to include another but instead, a dissolution of himself into a million parts of nothing: of a snowfall.

> scatter his nothing all over what angry skies and
> gently
>   (very whiteness:absolute peace,
> never imaginable mystery)
>   descend

[*Ps.*, no. 67]

I find that the echoes of the word "opening" in the entire preceding oeuvre now become almost unbearable to contemplate in the presence of this poem, and there could scarcely be a more powerful example of the way all of a poet's poems bear upon each. Most of all I thought of these stanzas from his loveliest lyric:

> your slightest look easily will unclose me
> though i have closed myself as fingers,
> you open always petal by petal myself as Spring opens
> (touching skilfully,mysteriously) her first rose
>
> ... ...
>
> (i do not know what it is about you that closes
> and opens;only something in me understands
> the voice of your eyes is deeper than all roses)
> nobody, not even the rain, has such small hands
>
> [*Ps.*, p. 263]

Notes

2. Linguists have noted that children create syntactic structures by the logic of deep structure rather than heard convention. Compare the following statement made by one of my young children:

> I want the muchest ice cream of Susannah.
> [I want as much ice cream as Susannah has.]

with Cummings' familiar first line:

> what if a much of a which of a wind
> gives the truth to summer's lie
>
> [*Ps.*, p. 401]

We are thrown back to where children are reliant again upon our natural possibilities of language and its underlying logic (Lyons, 1970), the combinatorial mathematics of which allow a child of fire "illimitably" (to borrow Cummings' word) to choose among more possible statements to utter than there are molecules in the universe:

> —when stars are hanged and oceans drowned,
> the single secret will still be man
>
> [*Ps.*, p. 401]

> —David V. Forrest, "E. E. Cummings and the Thoughts That Lie Too Deep for Tears: Of Defenses in Poetry," *Psychiatry* 43 (1980): 13, 14–15, 24, 29–30.

ROBERT K. JOHNSON ON THE POEM AS A REFLECTION OF CUMMINGS'S VIEW OF REALITY

[Robert K. Johnson is a retired Professor of English at Suffolk University and an acclaimed poet in his own right. Longtime host and founder of the Newton Free Library Poetry Series, his most recent collection is *Sudden Turnings* (2001). In this entry from the *Reference Guide to American Literature*, Johnson shows how the poem embodies Cummings' worldview.]

The bulk of E. E. Cummings's poetry falls into three major categories. He is perhaps most famous for his satirical poems, such as "Plato told" and "My sweet old etcetera." "All ignorance toboggans into know" is one of his many pieces that feature sweeping assertions. The third category consists of his poems of praise. He celebrates, for instance, the individualist in "My father moved through dooms of love"; the natural world in "This is the garden: colours come and go" and "In Just-"; the metaphysical world in "I will wade out"; and man's complexity in poems beginning "so many selves" and "but / he' i." Finally, "Somewhere i have never travelled, gladly beyond" exemplifies Cummings's many poems in praise of love. Because this poem also outlines Cummings's basic view of reality, it merits special attention.

The main reason the speaker in this love lyric values and praises his beloved so highly is introduced at the start of the poem when he states: "somewhere i have never travelled ... your eyes have their silence." For this "silence" leads the speaker to a richer knowledge of reality than his previous experiences did. Because this knowledge is wholly positive, both the speaker and the woman he loves react to it "gladly" or joyously. A fundamental feature of this deeper reality is gentleness—but a gentleness far more powerful than brute force. For this reason the beloved's "most frail gesture" spurs the speaker to seek being enclosed within the realm of love. Though the woman is physically attractive, the gentleness her beauty embodies also spurs the speaker beyond the solely sensual—beyond what he could "touch"—to "things" essentially metaphysical. Yet the metaphysical permeates physical reality. As Norman Friedman points out, the true world for Cummings is both "the natural world" and "a timeless world of the eternal present."

Stanza two makes it clear that the love awakened in the speaker is inclusive as well as exclusive. Although the speaker, it is implied, had previously closed himself off from a corrupt and hostile society, the woman he loves, symbolized by "Spring," opens him (a "rose") "petal by petal"—sexually, emotionally, spiritually. "Spring," the only word capitalized in the poem, not only stands for the beloved, but also connotes the most important characteristics of the material world—life and resurrection (connoting, in turn, eternity). Furthermore, the springtime is described as skillful and mysterious, indicating that love and nature have enormous, but unfathomable powers. In the third stanza's last two lines it is suggested again that the speaker's desire for exclusiveness is prompted by society's cruelty and crassness, represented by the snow "everywhere descending."

The penultimate stanza begins, "nothing which we are to perceive in this world equals / the power of your intense fragility." This fragility proves multifold, containing many "countries" or layers. The stanza's last line declares what was alluded to earlier. The power that resides within the woman renders "death and forever with each breathing." That is to say, quickened by love, the speaker intuits that physical reality and metaphysical reality are intertwined, and that the human spirit is immortal. Employing synesthesia in the last stanza, the speaker, re-emphasizes that although it permeates the material world, the timeless world is beyond rational comprehension. The speaker can say only that "something in me understands / the voice of your eyes is deeper than all roses." In the poem's last line, rain is personified. But "nobody, not even the rain, "has hands as "small" as his beloved's. For the speaker, nothing on earth matches the mysterious, delicate beauty of his beloved and of love.

"Somewhere i have never travelled, gladly beyond" is not a perfect representation of Cummings's poetry. It does not showcase the one original characteristic of his work, his experiments in word-coinage, punctuation, and typography—though he does in this poem use unconventional devices to prevent the punctuation from slowing down the rhythmic intensity. It is also true that Cummings's finest poems cannot hide the fact that his outlook on life became increasingly simplistic and intolerant. (In one poem he declares, "Humanity / i hate you.") However, "Somewhere i have never travelled, gladly beyond" does present Cummings's phrasing at its evocative best. Its content acknowledges life's painfulness, but promises that if people open themselves to love, they will gain the courage to withstand cruelty and will perceive the universe's immeasurably positive richness. Lastly, the poem contains Cummings's typical dynamic intensity, an intensity that pulls the reader along line by line.

—Robert K. Johnson, "'somewhere i have never traveled, gladly beyond': Poem by E. E. Cummings, 1931," *Reference Guide to American Literature*, 2nd. Ed. (Chicago, St. James Press, 1987): 682–83.

CRITICAL ANALYSIS OF
"my father moved through dooms of love"

Written in regular stanzas, with quatrains of iambic tetrameter, "my father moved through dooms of love" (*50 Poems*, 1940) has a deceptively conventional structure. It seems to fall neatly into four parts, the first three consisting of four stanzas each, and the last of five. These divisions are suggested by the periods at the ends of stanzas 4, 8, and 12; the capital letters beginning stanzas 5, 9, and 13; and the repetition of "my father moved" at the beginning of each section. This all seems perfectly logical until the reader hits the tone shift in stanza 14, a twist that might imply the poem has only two distinct sections: stanzas 1–13 serving as exposition, and 14–17 as kind of a coda or denouement.

Stretched across this customized framework is a thematic and syntactical fabric that provides the poem's true architecture. Allusions to natural phenomenon abound, and in each case follow an appropriately cyclical pattern. Most readily apparent is the poem's movement through the seasons, with the words "april," "midsummer," "septembering," "october," and then "spring" again, all falling in succession and with roughly even spacing. Sprinkled throughout this larger, annual cycle are words alluding to interconnected cycles in weather ("sun," "rain," "snow"), in landscape ("mountain," "valley," "sea"), and the daily cycle of "morning," "twilight," and "dark."

Seasonal shift is an extremely common theme in Cummings's work ("anyone lived in a pretty how town" is perhaps his most famous example), as are the primacy of Nature (e.g., "you shall above all things be glad and young") and the regenerative purity of spring ("in Just-" and "Spring is like a perhaps hand," among numerous others). A letter written by Cummings in 1959 attests to the fact that he even used the "seasonal metaphor" as an ordering principle in his poetry collections. As the letter also helps explain his transcendental intent, it is worth quoting at length (spaces have been added in some places to allow for easier reading):

"[I] seem to remember asserting that all my books of poems after the original T&C manuscript ... start with autumn (downgoing, despair) & pass through winter (mystery, dream) & stop in spring (upcoming, joy) ... *95 Poems* is, of course, an obvious example of the seasonal metaphor—1, a falling leaf; 41, snow; 73, nature (wholeness innocence eachness beauty the transcending of time & space) awakened. 'Metaphor' of what? Perhaps of whatever one frequently meets via my old friend S. Foster Damon's *William Blake/His Philosophy And Symbols*; e.g. (p 225) 'They' the angels 'descend on the material side ... and ascend on the spiritual; this is...a representation of the greatest Christian mystery, a statement of the secret which every mystic tries to tell'[.]"

—*Selected Letters of E. E. Cummings*, p. 261

Another deftly created, cyclic metaphor is expressed through the alternately deifying and humanizing descriptions of his father—a pattern that parallels the emotional vacillations within every parent-child relationship, but particularly the Oedipal drama that played out between E. E. and his father. Cummings's knowledge of Freudian theory is widely attested to, both in his own writings (the play *Him* is riddled with Freudian concepts) and those of his commentators (for the most thorough investigation, see Milton Cohen's essay "Cummings and Freud"). As Richard Kennedy reveals in *Dreams in the Mirror*, one of Cummings's early journal entries contains the explicit admission (concealed in his own shorthand): "I REVOLT ag[ainst] my F[ather]: would like TO KILL HIM." A few years after the actual death of his father, Cummings undertook a full psychoanalysis with a prominent disciple of Freud, Dr. Fritz Wittels, whom he described in his journals as the "poet of Freedom & Opening." Kennedy also states that the writing of "my father moved" was catalyzed by a "psychological breakthrough" that allowed Cummings to finally "identify himself with his father."

In the hands of a less-skilled poet, interweaving Nature and Freud might come off as forced or overdone, but thanks to Cummings's use of novel grammatical constructions and double-edged pairing of opposites, many of the thematic strands are more suggested than stated outright. As such, it might prove helpful to unravel the text section by section.

The opening stanza states the subject, establishes the meter and elegiac tone, and introduces a kind of poetic shorthand achieved by the pairings of opposites and the creation of new nouns from other parts of speech. By "moving" his father through "dooms of love," "haves of give," and "depths of height," Cummings portrays a dynamic, multidimensional individual who cannot be described by conventional adjectives or metaphors. He also conveys a large amount of information about his father's character in very few words. Simply by changing which word is emphasized, and exploring all the possible connotations of each pairing, an active reader can perceive a man who was doomed to love too much (a difficult son, sinful mankind), a man who had the means to be generous and felt the social responsibility to do so, and someone who experienced the highs and lows of an idealist in an imperfect world. Cummings had a name for this technique of augmenting a word with its opposite—he called it "knowing around." In his 1925 *Vanity Fair* essay, "You Aren't Mad, Am I?" (reprinted in *A Miscellany Revised*), Cummings traced the origins of this idea to several telling sources: a burlesque mime, modern art, and several works by Freud.

In our discussion of "All in green went my love riding" and "Memorabilia," we saw how Cummings used ambiguity and allusion to engage the reader. By studding the first stanza of "my father moved" with these multifaceted, attention-grabbing gems, Cummings has once again invited the reader to appraise his subject (and by extension, his poetry) from many angles at once, through a new lens of his or her own fashioning.

In the following stanza Cummings attributes his father with nothing less than the creation of the universe. This is not mere hyperbole—in the most basic biological sense Edward senior created Edward junior. He was also a Unitarian minister who believed that God was in every man. Moreover, he was poet, at least by the definition Cummings laid down in his foreword to *is 5*: "if a poet is anybody, he is somebody to whom things made matter very little—somebody who is obsessed by Making." In his roles as professor, minister, and father, Edward Cummings actively and creatively participated in the reshaping of the world he inhabited. In his son's worldview, everyone not involved in such a pursuit (occasionally dubbed "mostpeople" or "nonmakers") is an object of scorn and hardly merits the designation of a human being.

Subsequent stanzas continue the apotheosis, with stanza 6 making the charming claim that his father's heart was so pure that "a star by him could steer." Then, with the opening line of stanza 8, the reader gets the first intimations of humanity and mortality, appropriately followed by allusions to the more famous example of God made incarnate and Edward Cummings's analogous role as minister to the sick and the spiritually hungry. Stanza 9 assures the reader that he was neither a self-righteous windbag nor an unfeeling saint. In addition, line 35 in particular ("his anger was as right as rain") seems to contain a grown son's admission that he was often in the wrong. Stanzas 10-12 describe a man who, even in the face of old age and oncoming "dark," continued to live his life humbly and honorably. Stanza 13 provides a refrain of stanza 1 and returns the poem to its springtime starting point.

The abrupt tone shift in the next three and half stanzas ushers in a change in focus, away from the father and onto the bleak and comfortless world he "moved through." A point of grammar is worth noting here, as it will elucidate other examples in Cummings's oeuvre. Attentive readers may pause at the word "which" and wonder whether Cummings has made a mistake with his relative pronoun, but the usage is intentional, employed to dehumanize the "men" who "cannot share." Stanzas 15 and 16 continue the tour of hell, to the point where readers may begin to wonder if the narrator is going to strand them in the "mud and mire." But just as a word can be more precisely defined by being juxtaposed with its opposite, just as the night is darkest before the dawn, so too is the beauty of his father's example more finely etched by contrasting it with the greed and fear, doubt and conformity that dictate how most men live. Ultimately, the poem is about the redemptive power of a single life, a concept concisely summarized by the final couplet, in which the word "love" makes a telling reappearance. Far from being "doomed" by his love, Edward Cummings taught the world how to save itself.

"my father moved through dooms of love"

ORM ÖVERLAND ON TRANSCENDING THE PERSONAL

[Orm Överland is a Professor of American literature at the University of Bergen, Norway. He is the author of *The Western Home: A Literary History of Norwegian America, America Perceived: A View from Abroad in the Twentieth Century*, and *The American Home: A Literary History of Norwegian America*. In this condensation of his article on the poem, Overland traces how Cummings makes the leap from personal to universal expression.]

For the reader of the poetry of E. E. Cummings the main difficulty is frequently to understand the literal meaning of his verse. One reason is found in the poet's deliberate confusion of the conventional structural and lexical meanings of many of the words he employs. Once this screen is penetrated the poems appear to be both lucid and simple. Thus 'what a proud dreamhorse pulling (smoothloomingly) through' (p. 313)[1] may at first seem to be a mere jumble of words where the poet has played havoc with syntax beyond all reason, until one realizes that the poem consists of several interwoven sentences. The apparent disorder is not a mere joke on the reader but an attempt to convey an instant's spontaneous impression.

Cummings is thus often more bewildering than genuinely complex. One possible exception, however, is 'my father moved through dooms of love' (p. 373), which, along with its companion poem 'if there are any heavens my mother will (all by herself) have' (p. 253), ranks among the poet's highest achievements. It has a profusion of the grammatical oddities typical of Cummings. But beneath its bewildering surface there is a depth of feeling and sincerity of expression that is all too often lacking in the bulk of Cummings' work. Moreover, with its seventeen stanzas it is one of the longest of his poems. It thus offers an opportunity of examining the poet's ability to handle a somewhat more extended form than that of his usual brief lyrics. Although critics frequently have referred to 'my father moved' as one of Cummings' best poems, they nevertheless have had very little to say about it.[2]

The poem's point of departure is intensely personal—a devoted son's homage to his father. Although the poem succeeds in transcending the personal, the son is, nevertheless, Edward Estlin Cummings and the father Edward Cummings, minister of the South Congregational Church (Unitarian) and one time Professor of sociology at Harvard.[3] Cummings' love and reverence for his father as well as his mother have also found expression in his *i: Six Nonlectures*.[4] The first of these nonlectures, 'i & my parents', provides the reader with sufficient background to realize, had he ever been in doubt, that the poem has a sound basis in the poet's actual emotional attitude to his father.

'My father moved' has a regular stanza pattern, quatrains of iambic tetrameters. A fair number of lines begin with a trochee, and this slight variation of the meter serves to give the poem a peculiar singing quality—a quality not inappropriate to a hymn of praise. Working against the regularity of the rhythmic beat of the lines is the fairly systematic use of slant or imperfect rhyme, which serves to break a regularity that might otherwise have appeared monotonous. The verses may be sung out, as the poet seems to do, in defiance of the world, but they are not likely to lull you to sleep. (...)

In order to go beyond these mere surface observations, however, it is now necessary to consider the non-conventional linguistic structures that confront us in the opening stanza. The Cummingesque phrases 'dooms of love', 'sames of am', 'haves of give', and 'depths of height' are juxtapositions of words of contrasting connotations. In this context love connotes that which is capable of raising the human being above its doom or fate; being, human existence, is opposed to dead sameness. The meaning lies in the contemplation of these pairs of words as contrasted alternatives. The second word in each pair indicates the attainable ideal against which the lesser performances of 'mostpeople' are set off. For the first, second and fourth lines of stanza 1 are not descriptions of the father's world, the way he lived, but of the world he 'moved through', and this world of 'mostpeople' is a place where love is doomed, where existence is a drab repetition of movements, where possessions are held on to instead of being realized through being shared with others, and where the depths of this death-in-life existence, or unlife, are gauged by comparisons with the possible heights of true being: 'love', 'am', 'give'.

Besides suggesting a background against which the father's life must be seen, the opening stanza also presents the main image to be developed in the first section of the poem—that of the father as creator. The poet's father is able to sing into morning the night through which he moves, just as his mythological Father once created light out of darkness.[6] (Along with the obvious religious connotations of this image there is also a suggestion of the quite concrete image of a man who so to speak sings while he shaves, who can be approached safely in the morning before he has had his first cup of coffee.) This act of creation is associated with spring and the awakening of life brought about by the return of sun and warmth. The indeterminate 'where' that the father could bring into actual presence is 'motionless' in the sense that 'sames of am' is motionless; and 'forgetful' because it is not conscious of its past and, consequently, unaware of its possibilities. Such an existence 'is merely unlife until its drabness becomes 'shining here' before the father's glance. Confronted with his countenance lesser human beings could not long remain at peace with the many 'if's that stand between themselves and a full response to life.[7] The existence of 'where' or 'if' is not quite human, is the mode of existence of a mere 'which' as opposed to a 'who'. 'Which' is unburied because it is a death in life and because it is alive only in the negative sense that it is not yet buried. But, stirred by the warm sun of the father's eyes, this 'which' is capable of becoming 'who' or truly human.

The imagery of spring and of the father as the awakening influence is further developed in this third stanza. Under the father's influence human beings who had been asleep ('motionless forgetful') awaken to embrace their fates, their lives. This awakening is also to an awareness of their ghostly roots. On the concrete or literal level the roots of plants in spring may be ghostly in their whiteness. Here the image implies both the dreamers' history and their transcendental or spiritual roots. But for the awakening sleeper such a realization could well be ghostly also in the sense of being ghastly.[8]

On the first two lines of stanza 4 Theodore Spencer has commented: 'Substitute "girl" for "why" and an aura of pathos vanishes'. It may be added that the operation makes the lines well nigh meaningless in the bargain. For the 'why', though personalized as weak and feminine, is not a girl made more pathetic but the cry of the dreamer for whom the ghostly has indeed been too ghastly, and who questions the necessity of this brutal confrontation. The poet's father was clearly no relentless and insensitive idealist, who requires that the weak soul carry a load it cannot manage. Indeed, he is so sensitive he 'could feel the mountains grow' and lets the questioning soul return to sleep as a father would soothe a daughter awakened by a nightmare.

This brings us to the close of the first part of the poem. The dominant image has been that of the father as creator or life giver. Through the first three stanzas he has taken on the powers of a force in nature, being associated with the sun in spring defeating the waning influence of winter. In the fourth stanza, however, it is as if the poet has found it necessary to stress the virtue of his father's humanity in order to balance the scales. In the second section of the poem the image of the father as a god or celestial being is further developed; and a similar pattern of retraction may be observed in the eighth stanza as in the fourth.

Again the reader is reminded of the kind of world the poet sees his father surrounded by, here described as one which offers sorrow rather than its alternative, joy. Whether 'the valleys of the sea' may be thought of as the valleys at the bottom of the sea or the valleys between waves, they suggest depths, and the father's act of lifting them may be compared with his singing night into morning in the opening stanza. As in the first stanza this image also recalls the myth of Genesis when 'God said, Let the waters under the heaven be gathered together unto one place, and let the dry land appear'. The suggestion of the father as a superhuman force, a god-like figure whose existence is of an order raised high above that of lesser human beings, is made more explicit than in the previous sections. The sun-god-father is placed in the heavens along with the poet's mother in the female image of the moon (perhaps suggested by the lifting of the seas). The image of the father-sun praising the forehead of the mother-moon recalls the image of the two parents in the earlier poem, 'if there are any heavens my mother will (all by herself) have one':

> my father will be (deep like a rose
> tall like a rose)
>
> standing near my
>
> (swaying over her
> silent)
> with eyes which are really petals and see
>
> nothing with the face of a poet really which
> is a flower and not a face with
> hands
> which whisper
> This is my beloved my
>
>   (suddenly in sunlight
>
> he will bow,
>
> & the whole garden will bow)   (p. 253)

In the present poem, however, the image is not quite so formalized, it has more vitality, and procreation is an essential aspect of the father's love, 'singing desire into begin'.

While the image of the sun and moon may be slightly strained, to indicate the quality of the father's song of joy by suggesting that 'a heart of star by him could steer' is Cummings at his best. So pure was this joy, so present, alive and affirmative, that the poet imagines the very heavens rejoicing. Nevertheless, the banal is seldom far away even in the best of Cummings; here in the stock phrases 'heart of gold' and 'steer by a star' and in the celestial beings clapping hands for joy. Indeed, Cummings' technique very often consists of transforming banalities and clichés into art, literally making them new.

The movement of the second section has been from night (moon, star) through twilight to the full daylight of stanza 7. The brightness of day coincides with the mid-summer stage in the poem's movement through the seasons. Clearly this may be seen as a climax in the poem. But at this point the poem has come dangerously close to an anti-climax: the reader is bound to lose interest in a so too-good-to-be-true portrait of anyone's father, even Cummings'—and Cummings is obviously fully aware of this danger. The poem has been pointing towards an identification of the father with God/sun. But rather than an identification we now get a comparison, a simile. It is as if the poet has reminded us that this is poetry and that he has been giving us an image. Indeed, it is not the actual father, but his 'father's dream' that stood 'keen as midsummer's keen beyond / conceiving mind of sun will stand'. This dream of man and his possibilities is what ranges so high above the actual achievements of man. The poet's father is no exception. His own dream stood 'over utmost him so hugely'. The reader is thus prepared for the assertion made with full force in the concluding stanza of this section of the poem. The father was a man among men: 'his flesh was flesh his blood was blood'. After the poem has come dangerously close to making the father a god, there is this necessary retreat that parallels the strategy of the first part of the poem. Other men cannot but be drawn towards him, cannot but love him, not because he is superman but because he is human. Indeed, the father's Unitarian creed has found expression in the poet's assertion that it is in the full realization of his humanity that man is god-like.

This aspect of the father, his human quality, is the tenor of the third section of the poem. As he moved through 'dooms of love', he moves through a world where true feeling is doomed, where man is ruled by 'the pomp of must and shall' rather than by the directives of his own heart. By contrast, the father could be swayed by anger as well as pity.

What he had to offer the world was, in the final analysis, existence, being or true life as opposed to the 'unlife' of 'mostpeople' (to use two Cummingesque phrases from other poems); of his own abundance he 'offered immeasurable is' to the world of 'immeasurable happenless unnow'.[9]

The poem's movement through the cycle of seasons is now approaching the dead of winter. The father is indeed human. Though he is of that small minority (in Cummings' view) who are truly alive, he, too, must in the end succumb to death. The section which so strongly presents the father as a living man concludes with death and thus has a movement corresponding to that observed in the two first sections of assertion/retraction. But there is no defeat in this death: 'proudly ... / so naked for immortal work / his shoulders marched against the dark'. Neither does the poet consider this death as final. For the poem does not end in winter, but with the return of spring in stanza 13 introducing the fourth and last section of the poem:

> My father moved through theys of we,
> singing each new leaf out of each tree
> (and every child was sure that spring
> danced when she heard my father sing)

Inevitably, the father had to die, but with the return to spring there is the suggestion that all he did and stood for did not die with him.

The final stanzas evoke again the kind of world the poet's father. moved through, the world the poet in his moments of despair sees himself surrounded by, the worst of all possible worlds. It is a world where men kill rather than share (such men obviously do not qualify for the pronoun 'who'): where man is regarded as little more than 'mud and mire'; where there is cold scheming rather than imagination, passion merely something turned on and off at will, and freedom a state arrived at by the use of drugs; where stealing and cruelty have taken the place of charity and kindness, where people fear the directives of their own hearts and doubt their ability to think for themselves; where to be different is regarded as an aberration from the ideal of uniformity, and the pinnacle of being is conformity; where the bright has gone dull and the sweet bitter; where all there is to life is the prospect of final death; where no value is put on truth: indeed, where man lives for hate alone.

Even though the world had come to such extremes, the poet sums up his peroration,

> because my father lived his soul
> love is the whole and more than all

Thus the concluding couplet returns to the hope and promise of the spring images that introduced this last section. The memory of his father is still capable of bringing morning to the night of the contemporary world. (...)

In trying to find expression for his love as well as his admiration for his father Cummings created a vehicle that, perhaps more successfully than any of his other poems, brings forth his humanistic and individualistic ideals, his belief in the potential divinity of man which underlies his disgust with manunkind. Paradoxically, in the communication of the intensely private emotions of filial love E. E. Cummings' idiolect proves a universal language.

NOTES

* The editor regrets that extravagant conditions imposed by the publishers, Harcourt Brace Jovanovich, Inc., have prevented the inclusion of the text of the poem in the article as planned by the author.

1. Page references are to *Collected Poems* (New York, 1954).

2. See for instance George Haines IV, ': : 2 : 1—The World and E. E. Cummings'. *The Sewanee Review*, LIX (Spring 1951). 215–16; Theodore Spencer, 'Technique as Joy', in *E?TI: eec: E. E. Cummings and the Critics*, ed. S. V. Baum (East Lansing. Mich., 1962), p. 122; and Alfred Kazin, 'E. E. Cummings and his Fathers', *ibid.*, p. 187.

3. For further information on Edward Cummings see Richard S. Kennedy, 'Edward Cummings, the Father of the Poet', *Bulletin of the New York Public Library*, LXX (Sept. 1966), 437–49.

4. (Cambridge, Mass., 1966).

6. The association of Edward Cummings the father with God the Father is also present in the *nonlectures*: 'my father's voice was so magnificent that he was called on to impersonate God speaking from Beacon Hill (he was heard all over the common) ...' (pp. 8–9).

7. Compare the first three stanzas of No. 26 in *50 Poems*:

> wherelings whenlings / (daughters of ifbut offspring of
> hopefear / sons of unless and children of almost) / never
> shall guess the dimension of him whose / each / foot likes
> the / here of this earth whose both I eyes I love / this now
> of the sky (p. 367)

8. 'Rightly or wrongly, however, I prefer spiritual insomnia to psychic suicide. The hellless hell of compulsory heaven-on-earth emphatically isn't my pail of blueberries. By denying the past, which I respect, it negates the future— and I love the future.' (*i: Six Nonlectures*, p. 4).

9. For this last phrase see *Collected Poems*, p. 361.

—Orm Överland, "E. E. Cummings' 'my father moved through dooms of love': A Measure of Achievement, *English Studies* 54 (1952): 141–147.

RICHARD S. KENNEDY ON THE LIFE AND LEGACY OF EDWARD CUMMINGS

[A Professor Emeritus of English at Temple University and an original founder of the E. E. Cummings Society, Richard S. Kennedy is the author and editor of many publications on Cummings, including the seminal biography, *Dreams in the Mirror*. In this excerpt from an extended biographical essay, Kennedy examines the ways in which the poet was influenced by his father.]

Edward Cummings was the dominant figure in the early life of his son Edward Estlin Cummings, the poet, who was born October 14 1894. The man whom young Estlin knew during his childhood and youth, that is from about 1899 to 1916, was a tall (six feet one), broad-shouldered, brown-haired man with striking features including a prominent nose and a full moustache. He spoke with a resonant, authoritative voice. He was gay, informal, kindly but forcefully masculine in manner. Some of his pictures show him in handsome profile with resplendent waves of hair and with a black foulard tied in a flowing bow that makes him look like a poet who contributed to *The Yellow Book*. Other pictures show him in rugged, camper's clothes, like a Leslie Stephen ready to climb a mountain. These pictures represent two sides of his nature, for Edward Cummings was both a man of idea and a man of action.[1]

During the years when his son was growing up, Edward Cummings was the minister of the South Congregational Church, a Unitarian church at the corner of Exeter and Newbury, Streets in the fashionable Back Bay area of Boston. (...)

Cummings' creed is revealed very fully in a sermon he delivered on the general subject "Unitarianism, What It Means and What It Can Do under Existing Conditions for the Help of Mankind."[4] Cummings felt that a suitable definition and purpose of Unitarianism was "to promote the worship of God and the love and service of mankind in the spirit of Jesus." Although these words have the ring of nineteenth-century Unitarianism, Cummings felt that the church was not static but was in a constant state of becoming. He looked to the church of the future as a vital social instrument, "the church universal of world religion, world democracy, world peace." He saw Unitarianism as an outgrowth of the social message found in Christianity as well as in the other great religions and philosophies of the world: "The theology-weary world has been waiting for centuries, yes millenniums, for this practical religion of worship, love and service, in the spirit of Jesus. For his spirit is the spirit of all great truth-seekers and prophets; the spirit of Buddha and Socrates and Isaiah and Emerson.... Not the spirit of sacerdotalism or intolerance. But the spirit of truth; the, spirit of democracy; the family spirit of love and cooperation and devotion of strong to weak, which prevents weakness, and makes the weak strong and the strong stronger, and the world better and better without end." (...)

Edward Cummings' son, E. E. Cummings, the poet, did not see his father quite in the way I have described him. He saw him as the balanced, well-rounded man, to be sure, but he stressed details that show him less of an intellectual or spiritual leader and more of a manly kind of American hero—a combination of Daniel Boone and Benjamin Franklin:

He was a New Hampshire man, 6 foot 2,[20] a crack shot and a famous fly-fisherman & a firstrate sailor (his sloop was named The Actress) & a woodsman who could find his way through forests primeval without a compass & a canoeist who'd stillpaddle you up to a deer without ruffling the surface of a pond & an ornithologist & taxidermist & (when be gave up hunting) an expert photographer ... & an actor who portrayed Julius Caesar in Sanders Theatre & a painter (both in oils & watercolours) & a better carpenter than any professional & ... a plumber who just for the fun of it installed his own waterworks & (while at Harvard) a teacher with small use for professors—by whom (Royce, Lanman, Taussig, etc.) we were literally surrounded (but not defeated)—& later (at Doctor Hale's socalled South Congregational really

Unitarian Church) a preacher who announced, during the last war, that The Gott Mit Uns boys were in error since the only thing which mattered was for man to be on God's side ... & horribly shocked his pewholders by crying "the kingdom of Heaven is no spiritual roofgarden: it's inside you"[21] & my father had the first telephone in Cambridge & (Long before any Model T Ford) he piloted an Orient Buckboard with Friction Drive produced by the Waltham watch company & my father sent me to a certain public school because its principal was a gentle immense coal black negress ... & my father was a servant of the people who fought Boston's biggest & crookedest politician fiercely all day & a few evenings later sat down with him cheerfully at the Rotary Club & my father's voice was so magnificent that he was called on to impersonate God from Beacon Hill (he was heard all over the Common)....[22] (...)

Given this father–son situation, it is remarkable that young Cummings ever made much of a success of his life as a human being. He had a dominant, energetic father who mastered all the areas he entered, who would always be in stature a giant compared to his ordinary self, and who, note well, had a voice like God. It would seem a tremendous task for him to assert his own identity in the shadow of such a presence. But young Cummings did carry out a normal course of reaction against his father. He was irritated by many of his father's do-good activities, especially his membership in the Watch and Ward society and his temperance work. Later, when E. E. Cummings became the outspoken champion of individualism and the foe of group action, he was chopping away at his father's organizational approach to social problems and at his father's position as a socialist and a supporter of the political concept of one world. Also when he handled sexual situations with either mischief or unsparing frankness in his early poems, he was the minister's son dissociating himself from his father's image as a guardian of public morals.

Besides following this simple reaction pattern, young Cummings eventually achieved "self-actualization," as the psychologists say, by turning to important fields which his father had not conquered. He became a poet and a painter. (...)

But there are a few rather specific and important ways in which Edward Cummings helped to shape E. E. Cummings, the poet. Most prominent is the constant verbalization which was part of a minister's life. Then too, some of Edward Cummings' own habits of language were good for the ears of someone who was going to speak as a poet. He loved word-play. His sermons had puns, had toyings with proverbs and mottos and slogans, linguistic ways to attract or surprise the minds of his parishioners. ("Judge Actions by their People," "Worldliness is next to Godliness," "I want my church to be a layman's church," and so on.) He dealt liberally in metaphor and in large controling images. His sermon titles indicate it: "The Picture Puzzle of the Universe," "Mud Pies," "Spiritual Perennials." Much of this was a New England habit of mind, an emblematic view of the world we live in. But Edward Cummings went beyond it to create parables: "Invisible Barriers or the Bird in the Window," "The Parable of the Sugar Place" (a moral application of the process of maple-sugar-making), "The New Year Bank Account," "The Elevator or the Ups and Downs of Life," "The Railway Train Parable" (about the illusion of movement when you are standing still). When his son in later years wrote *Santa Clans, A Morality*, he was following, and surpassing, his father's practice. (...)

Edward Cummings is [also] partly responsible for a world-view which occasionally emerges in E. E. Cummings' poems. It is a combination of humanism and natural religion that is distinctly Unitarian in coloration because the celebration of man and the appreciation of the natural world are the two most outstanding features of Unitarianism. This appears in such poems and lines as "i thank You God for most this amazing / day," "in Spring comes (no one asks his name) a mender of things," "the single secret will still be man," "from spiralling ecstatically this / proud nowhere of earth's most prodigious night / blossoms a newborn babe"—besides the numerous poetic acknowledgments of leaves, flowers, stars, children, and other everyday miracles of creation. (...)

[Edward Cummings] has more than one memorial. In the Hale Memorial Chapel of the First Church, a bronze tablet with a bas relief, a half-figure in profile, describes him simply: "Teacher. Preacher. Peacemaker." In Silver Lake, New Hampshire, a tall, cone-shaped lighthouse, built of lakestone, which stands at the head of Silver Lake, was erected by the townsfolk in his memory. They had never considered Cummings "summer people." But the best known memorial is the long tribute by his son, "my father moved through dooms of love," which rises in climax to this conclusion:

> My father moved through theys of we,
> singing each new leaf out of each tree
> (and every child was sure that spring
> danced when she heard my father sing)
>
> then let men kill which cannot share,
> let blood and flesh be mud and mire,
> scheming imagine, passion willed,
> freedom a drug that's bought and sold ...
>
> though dull were all we taste as bright
> bitter all utterly things sweet,
> maggoty minus and dumb death
> all we inherit, all bequeath
>
> and nothing quite so least as truth
> —I say though hate were why men breathe—
> because my father lived his soul
> love is the whole and more than all[25]

NOTES

1. Information about the life of Edward Cummings in this study is drawn from a press release by the South Congregational Church published in the Boston *Transcript* and the Boston *Herald*, August 21 1900; newspaper accounts in the Woburn *News*, August 21 1900, Boston *Advertiser*, October 8 1900, and Boston *Herald*, November 21 1913; a newspaper interview by Edith Talbot, July 8 1916, and other newspaper clippings in the Harvard University Archives; manuscript materials in the possession of Mrs E. E. Cummings; the *Unitarian Year Book*, 1927–28; and interviews with Mrs. Carlton Qualey (Elizabeth Cummings), Dr Rhys Williams, and Dr James Silbey Watson. I am deeply grateful to Mrs E. E. Cummings for allowing me to examine and make excerpts from the notes and sermons of Edward Cummings.

4. *The Layman's Answer*.

20. Note that he adds an inch to his father's height.

21. In Sermon 69 "New Heaven and New Earth," Edward Cummings told his hearers: "Now timid people do not enjoy having the old heaven and the old earth pass away.... The old-fashioned three-story universe just suited them.... There was a hell in the basement for their enemies and the enemies of God; there was a heavenly roof-garden for themselves and their friends on top; and

the earth was a sort of recruiting station halfway between the two." Also he preached Sermon 22, May 19 1901, "The Kingdom of God Is Within You."

22. From a letter to Paul Rosenfeld which E. E. Cummings quoted in *I: Six Non-Lectures* (Cambridge, Mass, 1953), Non-lecture One, "i & my parents."

25. From "my father moved through dooms of love" in *Poems 1923–1954* by E. E. Cummings, copyright, 1940, by E. E. Cummings. Reprinted by permission of Harcourt, Brace and World, Inc.

—Richard S. Kennedy, "Edward Cummings, the Father of the Poet," *New York Public Library Bulletin* 70 (1966): 437–438, 441, 445–449.

ROBERT E. MAURER ON CUMMINGS'S INDIVIDUALIST SYNTAX

[Robert E. Maurer wrote his doctoral dissertation on Cummings and has published numerous articles on contemporary literature. For a number of years, he taught American Literature at Antioch College; he has also written for *Current Biography*. In this article excerpt, Maurer analyzes the poet's trademark reinvention of simple words like "if" and "why."]

To refer to Cummings' words as nouns and verbs is to make things sound much simpler than they are, for the one outstanding characteristic of his mature style is his disrespect for the part of speech. It would be more accurate instead to say that he *uses* words as nouns, for instance, which are not normally so; it would be hard to find any one of his later poems which does not utilize a word in a sense other than its usual one. *Yes* is used as a noun to represent all that is positive and therefore admirable, *if* to stand for all that is hesitating, uncertain, incomplete. The style thus becomes spare; the later books contain many poems written in extremely short lines, lines which, utilizing the simplest words, say a great deal. For instance, these two fragments from *1 x 1*:

> yes is a pleasant country:
> if's wintry
> (my lovely)
> let's open the year   (from XXXVIII: 412)

who younger than
begin
are,the worlds move
in your
(and rest,my love)
honour   (from XXXV: 410)

    It is possible, of course, to argue that in the above stanzas *yes*, *if*, and *begin* do not convey precise meanings; that, since they are not used within their historical framework, no one but the poet can possibly know exactly what he meant to convey. This is an objection that, if it is accepted, is unanswerable; and the person who reads with such an assumption by his side will never make any sense out of Cummings' poems. But again, by accepting the fact that the poet may be saying something worthwhile and may be seriously trying to convey both truth and beauty as he sees it, one will try to look through the poet's eyes. To understand Cummings fully, more so than in understanding most other poets, it is necessary for one to have read much of Cummings. To a reader familiar with his techniques such a statement as "yes is a pleasant country" is as penetrable as a deep, clear pool; it might, however, seem more opaque to one reading him for the first time. Such words as *yes* and *if* take on a historical meaning within the body of his poetry, a meaning not divorced from their traditional ones but infinitely larger: *yes*, for instance, conventionally is used in a particular situation; as Cummings uses it, *yes* represents the sum of all the situations in which it might be used. And such a technique as "who younger than / begin / are" is not too complicated to be used by some practitioners of the art of writing for mass consumption, as witness the first line of a very popular song from *South Pacific*: "Younger than springtime, you are."

    One of Cummings' most universally liked poems, "my father moved through dooms of love" (*50 POEMS*, 34: 373–5), is extremely dense linguistically as a result of its suffusion with such words as *sames, am, haves, give, where, here, which, who, why, begin, pure, now, beyond, must*, and *shall* used as nouns. Again, it is helpful, if not necessary, to know the basic assumptions of Cummings, to know what he likes and what he dislikes, in order to interpret these reincarnated words. The following couplet will serve as an example:

> and should some why completely weep
> my father's fingers brought her sleep: (p. 374)

A word such as *why* in an otherwise simple, straightforward passage such as this calls attention to itself at once; it causes a linguistic shock. Its startling effect is not due merely to the fact that it is used as a noun, since *why* does sometimes function in this fashion, in such expressions as "get to the *why* (bottom) of the situation," or "there is a terrible *why* (enigma) involved in this." However, it is immediately obvious that such normal substantive meanings of the word are not called into play in Cummings' couplet, and the reader must use his own resourcefulness in exploring the possibilities of new meaning.

In these two particular lines *why* actually presents no difficulty, for it is placed in the context of a concrete dramatic situation that is perfectly understandable: the *her* in the second line indicates that *why* is the substantive antecedent of the pronoun and that it can therefore be assumed to represent some feminine noun of a general character, such as *girl* or *woman*. If, however, *girl* or *woman* should be substituted for *why*, the startling quality of the first line would surely be lost, as would much of Cummings' meaning, which is ascertainable as much from the nature of the word *why* itself as from its use in context. In normal interrogative usage *why* presupposes an unanswered question and a mind searching for answers. If these conditions are fitted into the dramatic situation that is portrayed in the couplet—a girl weeping and given peace through sleep—the elements fit together: she is mentally puzzled, unable to answer the questions in her mind, miserable because she is mixed up. So that without further extensions the passage conveys an exact meaning, if not all that Cummings intended.

Just as do *yes*, *if*, and *begin* in the passages quoted above, *why* takes on an aura of meaning within the body of his poetry, a meaning that it is impossible to illustrate from this single example. Babette Deutsch has described Cummings' use of these words as follows:

> His later poems make words as abstract as "am," "if," "because," do duty for seemingly more solid nouns. By this very process, however, he restores life to dying concepts. "Am" implies being at its most responsive, "if" generally means the creeping timidity

that kills responsiveness, and "because" the logic of the categoriz-
ing mind that destroys what it dissects. Here is a new vocabulary,
a kind of imageless metaphor.[15]

Why, Miss Deutsch might further have explained, generally
means to Cummings a state of uncertainty, a searching for
direction from sources outside oneself, an unspontaneous
demanding of reasons and causes in the face of life. A person who
is a *why* is generally a subject for ridicule, being, like an *if*, a timid
creature who thinks, fears, denies, follows, unlike an all-alive *is*.
However, in the couplet above the measure of Cummings'
father's compassion and stature is that he sees this particular *why*
as a pitiful creature, to whom he brings solace through love.

NOTE

15. *Poetry in Our Time* (New York, 1952), p. 113.

> —Robert E. Maurer, "Latter-Day Notes on E. E. Cummings'
> Language," *E. E. Cummings: A Collection of Critical Essays*, Norman
> Friedman, ed. (Englewood Cliffs: Prentice-Hall, 1972): 90–92.

RUSHWORTH M. KIDDER ON REDEMPTION AND THE HEROIC INDIVIDUAL

> [In this selection from his book on Cummings's poetry,
> Kidder peels away the poem's "smooth façade" to reveal
> the recondite meaning hiding beneath.]

The world, in "my father moved through dooms of love" (34),
needs redemption: it is a place of "scheming" and "passion," of
stealing, cruelty, fear, and doubt, and of "maggoty minus and
dumb death." Unlike some of Cummings' poems, however, this
one emphasizes not primarily this corruption but the nature of
the individual who redeems it. And unlike other poems, this one
presents an individual who finds answers not in transcendent
escape but in direct engagement and correction of the world's
wrong. It is a poem about love. But like the Gospels—in which
the word "love" appears with surprising infrequency—the poem
does not so much explain as demonstrate. Defining the attributes
of love not in exposition but through narrative, it echoes the

technique of the Gospel writers by showing how love is exemplified in the works of a single man. Fittingly, the word "love" occurs only twice in the poem—in the first and last lines.

Commentators have generally assumed that the poem is biographical. That Cummings had deep respect for his own father is born out by their voluminous correspondence in the decade between Cummings' graduation and his father's death in 1926. Too independent to be merely submissive, and too affectionate to be merely rebellious, Cummings shows himself sometimes bemused at his father's advice, sometimes bristling at its implications, and consistently friendly and appreciative. The tone of the letters resembles that of the affectionate portrait of his father in Cummings' first Harvard non-lecture in 1953. There he elevates his father to the status of Renaissance man, marking first his skills in the practical arts ("a crack shot & a famous fly-fisherman," a woodsman, taxidermist, carpenter, and plumber) and then his talents as professor, preacher, and public servant. Noting that acting was one of his hobbies, he observes that "my father's voice was so magnificent that he was called on to impersonate God speaking from Beacon Hill." The father in the lecture and the poem is indeed a godlike man. But whether he is more closely allied to the real-life model than any of America's folk heroes are to their originals is a matter best left to biographers. Certainly the poem describes in some ways the Reverend Edward Cummings. Essentially, however, it describes qualities of feeling and habits of mind which have fathered Cummings' own mental set. Not simply recording the ideals of a real man, the poet chooses to embody his own highest ideals in a fictionalized character, describe him in action, and claim a sonship with him which makes clear his own intellectual and spiritual heritage.

This lower-case poem is divided into four parts, each marked with an initial capital. But, like a fifteen-line sonnet—and like its larger-than-life hero—the poem exceeds itself, and is perhaps best described as a sixteen-stanza piece that has seventeen stanzas. The first three groups of four stanzas blend seasonal reference (from "april" through "midsummer's" into "octobering") with images of growth (from birth through strength and into harvest). The first stanza of each of these parts defines what his father moved through and sets out the subjects for the stanzas immediately following: "dooms of love" (stanza one), "griefs of joy" (stanza five), and "dooms of feel" (stanza nine). In each part, three stanzas describe the father, while the fourth focuses on his effect on those around him. Toward the end of the third part the seasonal metaphor accelerates: the harvest imagery of stanza 12 ends with the "snow" of winter. By stanza 13—the beginning of the fourth part, in which we might have expected winter imagery—spring has already come. The strategy then shifts quickly, reducing the description of his father to one stanza and following it by the four-stanza climax which, delineating the characteristics of the world he wars against, ultimates in grand affirmation.

Where some of Cummings' poems are aggressively complex and others patently simple, this one erects a smooth facade which, significant in itself, reverberates inside with more profound meaning. Apparently simple, it nevertheless rewards close reading. The phrase "moved through," as Lane rightly notes, "means 'travelled amidst,' 'passed beyond,' 'was animated by,' and 'expressed himself by means of.'" So "my father moved through dooms of love" suggests not only that he espoused love as his fate or fortune but also that he overcame the notion of love as his demise. Similar multiplicity of meaning surrounds "sames of am," "haves of give," and "depths of height," each of which can mean something positive which he welcomes and something negative which he resists: "sames of am," for example, suggests both a slavish conformity and a wonderful consistency, one of which he would overcome and the other embrace. In his presence, "this ... where" turns to "here," and "that if" (a conditional sense of things which is "so timid" that by contrast "air is firm") begins to "stir" with life. His "april touch" awakens the lethargic and comforts the sorrowing: and "no smallest voice" would cry in vain (and, as Lane observes, with vanity) to this man who, one with nature, redeems the meek while deflating the proud. A story of creation, the first stanzas parallel Genesis while overturning *The Waste Land*. Assembling a number of words echoing the first six lines of Eliot's poem ("forgetful," "stir," "april," "roots," "unburied," and "sleeping"), Cummings reverses the thrust of Eliot's despair and restores April to its more traditional place. With stanzas 14 the poet shifts into a denser syntax. As though to slow us down and insist on our attentiveness—as though to prevent us from hastening in with our own preconceptions about meaning—Cummings describes the world of evil in a compact and eliptical style:

> then let men kill which cannot share,
> let blood and flesh be mud and mire,
> scheming imagine,passion willed,
> freedom a drug that's bought and sold
>
> giving to steal and cruel kind
> a heart to fear,to doubt a mind....

The first couplet is clear. Thereafter words must be inserted regularly: let men, scheming and willed by passion, imagine that freedom is a drug; let them imagine that giving is to steal, that cruel is kind, that a heart is made to fear and a mind made to doubt. Let them imagine that the world is really as bad as the poet described it in "as freedom is a breakfastfood" (25) or "(of Ever-Ever Land i speak" (*New Poems*, 4). Let them imagine what they will: for "though hate were why men breathe"—the summary phrase for these lesser and more specific evils—the point is not these imagined lies but the reality of love. It is not an abstract love. It is not, as it was not in the poem to his mother ("if there are any heavens," *ViVa*, XLII), a "pansy heaven." It is a love embodied in the works of a man who "lived his soul," not of those who, like the townspeople in "anyone lived in a pretty how town," "slept their dream." Not the stuff of romantic attachments, it is the love which, in the New Testament, is the basis of Christianity and which is the only explanation for the events reported there. Here, as there, the validation for the final absolute statement—"love is the whole and more than all"—is the particularity of the life already described.

—Rushworth M. Kidder, *E. E. Cummings: An Introduction to the Poetry* (New York: Columbia University Press, 1979): 147–150.

JAMES P. DOUGHERTY ON THE THIRD POETIC WORLD

[James P. Dougherty is a Professor of English at the University of Notre Dame. He is the author of *Walt Whitman and the Citizen's Eye* and *The Fivesquare City*, as well as the creator of *PoemReader*, a hypertext tutorial. In this article excerpt, Dougherty places a spotlight on Cummings's syntactical high wire act.]

The perennial problem for the Imagist is the transition from experience to significance—the need, as Williams said at the beginning of *Paterson*, "to make a start / out of particulars / and make them general." Symbolic realism, in which an object is cumulatively charged with meaning through the terms and limits its description and through direct commentary—in which two farmers mending a wall become types of two complex attitudes toward definition and limitation—was evidently not congenial to Cummings, for he seldom attempts this transition. Either his poems imitate the disorder of pure phenomena, or else take form from the development of a general observation proceeding from his neo-romantic philosophy of primitivist, anti-intellectual vitalism. This division corresponds generally with the division of his work into poems for the eye, which because of their typographic irregularity can be comprehended only visually, and poems for the ear, which can be both read and spoken. Among the latter are "pity this busy monster, manunkind," "my father moved through dooms of love," and "anyone lived in a pretty how town"—some of his best-known poems.[6] What constitutes "the concrete" in them is interesting. (...)

All three poems, especially the last two, depend for their immediacy on Cummings' unusually developed sense of the reality of a third poetic world, neither that of material objects nor that of immaterial significances but that of language itself—words, their orthography and grammar—a world so obvious that most theories of the particular and the general in poetry ignore it altogether.[8] Cummings is in this sense an anti-nominalist, an extreme realist, for whom words themselves have important concrete reality both in sound and in physical extension. His typographic poems develop out of this sense that a written word is a set of printed characters that can be pried apart to reveal new words, or distributed on the page so as to coerce the eye and the mind into special rhythms of comprehension. His sense of sound is responsible for such arrangements as "death and life safely beyond" in the "manunkind" poem, or, in the elegy to his father, "keen as midsummer's keen beyond / conceiving: mind of sun," in which a compound adjective, "keen beyond mind's conceiving" is reorganized for the sake of sound and rhythm. Of course, in disturbing syntax to create euphonies, rhymes or rhythms, Cummings is balancing near the edge of the technical self-indulgence that has reduced the coherence—and hence the stature—of many of his poems. But he risks this because of his confident orientation in the universe of English structure and his confidence that the same familiarity with their language has given his readers better sea legs than they know. Elsewhere he preserves syntactical pattern and normal inflections as a guide to the reader, while substituting his own neologisms: "he sang his didn't he danced his did"; "my father moved through theys of we." The technique is familiar from Lewis Carroll.

But the result is not like Carroll's, for the neologisms are not private nonce words like "snark" and "toves," whose meanings we guess from the context of the one poem, but familiar public words like "they" and "did," whose meaning we establish by considering the situations in which they are normally used in the total context of our language. An easy example, from the elegy to his father, is

> newly as from unburied which
> floats the first who,his april touch
> drove sleeping selves to swarm their fates

We comprehend "which" as a metaphor for "some inanimate thing" and "who" as "a human person," because we are familiar with the assignments of these terms in our normal speech. Yet the unusual thing about these metaphors is that the vehicle in each case, instead of being a definite, concrete, and sensory thing, is just a function-word, without any corresponding object in reality. Each is a metonymy, founded on syntactics rather than semantics, representing an object not by another *object* associated with Ii (as "pen" for "poetry"), but by a *word* associated with it. Here too, writer and reader depend upon an intense realization of the system of language, distinct from the world of entities to which language refers. The reader experiences the pleasure of wit, of negotiating the transfer from vehicle to tenor, of seeing what was not stated, but the metaphor does not illuminate for him a hitherto unapprehended connection between actual things, as Shelley thought it must, but rather between a word in itself and a general class of things.

The same practice can be found throughout "my father moved through dooms of love" and the metaphors are not always so obvious as "which" and "who." In the opening lines-"my father moved through dooms of love / through sames of am through haves of give," the pattern "through x of y" is three times repeated, but only gradually the relationship of its two terms becomes clear, that x is what must be risked if y is to be attained. We can establish this by a general familiarity with how "same" is related (for Cummings) to "am"; and "have" to "give" and "they" to "we."

What emerges from the elegy is a parable, presenting his father as a creative, dynamic man dedicated to increasing the joy and vitality of his neighbors. It is a parable without episodes, without particular details; it is not about Edward Cummings, Harvard '83, who lived at 104 Irving Street in Cambridge and died in 1926, fourteen years before this poem was published; like the other poem, it is about "anyone": anyone who meets the poet's definition of true humanity. Yet we acknowledge that "my father moved through theys of we / singing each new leaf out of each tree" has an immediacy, a precision, that would not exist in a paraphrase such as "any man, seeking to impress his love for other men and his sense of physical participation in the natural world, exposes himself to grave risks of rejection, alienation and failure, risks which must be embraced to be overcome." It is not that the paraphrase lacks accuracy or completeness of statement, but that it wants intensity and organization of sound. (...)

Thus, In the three idea-poems we have considered, there is a progressively greater departure from the phenomenological world of definite persons, things, and actions. This is the world in which most modern poets have rooted themselves, in order to escape the intangible, unaffective and imprecise language of abstraction. Cummings is capable of depicting this physical world with hypersensitive accuracy in his "immediate" poems, and sometimes capable of using it for such conceits as "electrons deify one razorblade ..." or for the seasonal references ("sun moon stars rain") which tie so many of his poems to the definite. But he is seldom able to move, within one poem, from the phenomenal world to developed general discourse, and herein lies one of his limitations as a poet. In some of his best-known and most ambitious poems, he is writing a tissue of abstractions or generalizations, vivified not so much by tangible symbols as by an appeal to the tangibility of language itself. First, by a peculiar conviction of the reality of a universe of language, in which one can depict the unwishes of unpeople, in which "magical omnipotence" can be wound up one more turn to "hypermagical ultraomnipotence," and in which great liberties with customary grammar are taken in the knowledge that his reader's resources of comprehension have been developed but never fully exploited by his normal reading. Second, his generalizing poems are made vivid by his unusual awareness of the concrete reality of words themselves, occupying physical space on the printed page and, when artistically distributed, directing the eye in mimetic rhythms; or creating certain patterns of sound and syntax which often are repeated until their grammatical function is submerged in their audial reality. In Cummings' poems of statement, we can sometimes praise the wit, or even the vision, of his sentences. But we must always look to the cunning, vivid texture of verbal arrangements and of the words taken as realities in themselves.

NOTES

6. *Poems 1923–1954* (New York: Harcourt, Brace, 1954), pp. 397, 373–75, 370–71.

8. Connotation and denotation, tenor and vehicle, intension and extension, concrete and universal, etc. René Wellek, in "The Mode of Existence of a Literary Work of Art," in *Theory of Literature* (New York: Harcourt, Brace, & World, 1965), does acknowledge a "sound-stratum" and a "syntactic structure" before proceeding to higher things.

> —James P. Dougherty, "Language as a Reality in E. E. Cummings," *Critical Essays on E. E. Cummings*. Ed. Guy Rotella, (Boston, G.K. Hall & Co., 1984): 185–187, 190–191.

WORKS BY

E. E. Cummings

Eight Harvard Poets, 1917.
The Enormous Room, 1922.
Tulips and Chimneys, 1923.
&, 1925.
XLI Poems, 1925.
Is 5, 1926.
Him, 1927.
[No Title], 1930.
CIOPW, 1931.
ViVa, 1931.
The Red Front, 1933.
Eimi, 1933.
No Thanks, 1935.
Tom, 1935.
Collected Poems, 1938.
50 Poems, 1940.
1 x 1, 1944.
Santa Claus, 1946.
Xaipe, 1950.
i: six nonlectures, 1953.
Poems 1923-1954, 1954.
A Miscellany, 1958.
95 Poems, 1958.
Adventures in Value, 1962.
73 Poems, 1963.
Fairy Tales, 1965.
A Miscellany Revised, 1965.
Three Plays and a Ballet, 1968.
Selected Letters of E. E. Cummings, 1969.
Complete Poems 1923-1962, 1972.
Poems 1905-1962, 1973.
Etcetera: The Unpublished Poems of E. E. Cummings, 1983.
Complete Poems 1904-1962, 1991.
*Pound / Cummings: The Correspondence of Ezra Pound and
    E. E. Cummings*, 1996.
AnOther E. E. Cummings, 1998.

WORKS ABOUT
E. E. Cummings

Barton, Cynthia. "Cummings' 'Memorabilia,'" *The Explicator* 22 (1963): Item 26.

Baum, Stanley V. *ESTI: e e c; E. E. Cummings and the Critics*. East Lansing: Michigan State UP, 1962.

Belouf, Robert L. *E. E. Cummings: the Prosodic Shape of his Poems*. Diss. Northwestern University, 1954. Ann Arbor: UMI, 1978.

Cohen, Milton. "Cummings and Freud," *American Literature* 55:4 (1983): 591–610.

———. *POETandPAINTER: The Aesthetics of E. E. Cummings's Early Work*. Detroit: Wayne State UP, 1987.

———. "The Dial's 'White-Haired Boy': E. E. Cummings as *Dial* Artist, Poet, and Essayist," *Spring* 1 (1992): 9–27.

Collins, Michael J. "Formal Allusion in Modern Poetry," *Concerning Poetry* 9:1 (1976): 5–12.

Cowley, Malcolm. "Cummings: One Man Alone," *Yale Review* 62:3 (1973): 332–354.

Cureton, Richard D. "Poetry, Grammar, and Epistemology: The Order of Prenominal Modifiers in the Poetry of E. E. Cummings," *Language & Style* 18:1 (1985): 64–91.

———. "Visual Form in E. E. Cummings': *No Thanks*," *Word & Image* 2:3 (1986): 245–77.

Davenport, Guy. "Transcendental Satyr." *Every Force Evolves a Form*. San Francisco: North Point (1987): 29–36.

Davis, William V. "Cummings' 'All in green went my love riding,'" *Concerning Poetry* 3 (1970): 65–67.

Dendinger, Lloyd, ed. *E. E. Cummings: The Critical Reception*. New York: Burt Franklin & Co., 1981.

Dumas, Bethany K. *E. E. Cummings: A Remembrance of Miracles*. London: Vision Press, 1974.

Eckley, Wilton. *The Merrill Guide to E. E. Cummings*. Columbus: Charles E. Merrill, 1970.

————. *The Merrill Checklist of E. E. Cummings*. Columbus: Charles E. Merrill, 1970.

Everson, Edith A. "E. E. Cummings' Concept of Death," *Journal of Modern Literature* 7:2 (1979): 243–254.

Fairley, Irene R. "Cummings' Love Lyrics: Some Notes by a Female Linguist," *Journal of Modern Literature* 7:2 (1979): 205–218.

————. *E. E. Cummings and Ungrammar.* New York: Watermill. 1975.

Finn, H. Seth. "Cummings' 'Memorabilia,'" *Explicator* 29 (1971): Item 42.

Firmage, George J. *E. E. Cummings: A Bibliography*. Middletown: Wesleyan University Press, 1960.

Forrest, David V. "E. E. Cummings and the Thoughts That Lie Too Deep for Tears: Of Defenses in Poetry," *Psychiatry*, 43 (1980).

————. "A First Look at the Dreams of E. E. Cummings: The Preconscious of a Synthetic Genius," *Spring* 2 (1993): 8–19.

Friedman, Norman. *E. E. Cummings: The Art of His Poetry*. Baltimore: the Johns Hopkins Press, 1960.

————. *E. E. Cummings: The Growth of a Writer*. Carbondale: Southern Illinois UP, 1964.

————. *E. E. Cummings: A Collection of Critical Essays*. Englewood Cliffs: Prentice-Hall, 1972.

————. *(Re)Valuing Cummings: Further Essays on the Poet, 1962–1993*. Gainesville: University Press of Florida, 1996

Funkhouser, Linda Bradley. "Acoustical Rhythms in Cummings' 'Buffalo Bill's,'" *Journal of Modern Literature* 7:2 (1979): 219–242.

Gerber, Philip L. "E. E. Cummings's Season of the Censor," *Contemporary Literature* 29:2 (1988): 177–200.

Haines, George. "2:1—The World and E.E. Cummings," *Sewanee Review* 59 (1951): 206–227.

Headrick, Paul. "'Brilliant Obscurity': The Reception of *The Enormous Room*," *Spring* 1 (1992): 46–76.

Heusser, Martin. *I Am My Writing: The Poetry of E. E. Cummings*. Tubingen: Stauffenburg Verlag, 1997

Johnson, Robert K. "'somewhere I have never traveled, gladly beyond': Poem by E. E. Cummings, 1931," *Reference Guide to American Literature, 2nd. Ed.* (Chicago, St. James Press, 1987): 682–83.

Jumper, Will C. "Cummings' 'All in green went my love riding,'" *Explicator* 26:6 (1967): Item 6.

Kennedy, Richard S. "Edward Cummings, the Father of the Poet," *New York Public Library Bulletin* 70 (1966): 437–449.

———. "E. E. Cummings: The Emergent Styles, 1916," *Journal of Modern Literature* 7:2 (1979): 175–204.

———. *Dreams in the Mirror: A Biography of E. E. Cummings*. New York: Liveright Pub. Corp., 1980.

———. *E. E. Cummings Revisited*. New York: Twayne Publishers, 1994.

Kidder, Rushworth M. *E. E. Cummings: An Introduction to the Poetry*. New York: Columbia UP, 1979.

———. "Cummings and Cubism: The Influence of the Visual Arts on Cummings' Poetry," *Journal of Modern Literature* 7:2 (1979): 255–291

———. "Picture into Poem: the Genesis of Cummings's '*i am a little church*,'" *Contemporary Literature* 21:3 (1980): 315–330.

Kilby, Clyde S. "Cummings' 'Memorabilia,'" *Explicator* 12:2 (1953): Item 15.

Lane, Gary. *I Am: A Study of E. E. Cummings' Poems*. Lawrence: The University Press of Kansas, 1976.

Lauter, Paul. *E. E. Cummings: Index to First Lines and Bibliography of Works By and About the Poet*. Denver: Alan Swallow, 1955.

Logan, John. "The Organ Grinder and the Cockatoo: An Introduction to E. E. Cummings," *Modern American Poetry: Essays in Criticism*, Ed. Jerome Mazzaro. (New York: David McKay, 1970): 249–271.

Marks, Barry M. *E. E. Cummings*. New York: Twayne Publishers, 1964.

McBride, Katherine Winters. *A Concordance to the Complete Poems of E. E. Cummings*. Ithaca: Cornell University Press, 1989.

Miller, Lewis H., Jr. "Advertising in Poetry: A Reading of E. E. Cummings' 'POEM, OR BEAUTY HURTS MR. VINAL'," *Word & Image* 2:4 (1986): 349–62.

Norman, Charles. *The Magic-Maker: E. E. Cummings*. New York: Macmillan, 1958.

Överland, Orm. "E. E. Cummings' 'my father moved through dooms of love': A Measure of Achievement," *English Studies* 54 (1952): 141–147.

Ray, David. "The Irony of E.E. Cummings," *College English* 23:4 (1962): 282–290.

Robey, Cora. "Cummings' 'All in green went my love riding,'" *Explicator* 27:1 (1968): Item 2.

Rotella, Guy L. *E. E. Cummings: A Reference Guide*. Boston: Hall, 1979.

Rotella, Guy, ed. *Critical Essays on E. E. Cummings*. Boston: G. K. Hall & Co, 1984.

Sanders, Barry. "Cummings' 'All in green went my love riding,'" *Explicator* 25:3 (1966): Item 23.

Thompson, William E. "Intensity: An Essential Element in E. E. Cummings' Aesthetic Theory and Practice," *University of Windsor Review*, 16:2 (1982): 18–33.

Triem, Eve. *E. E. Cummings*. Minneapolis: University of Minnesota, 1969.

Van Peer, Willie. "Top-Down and Bottom-Up: Interpretative Strategies in Reading E. E. Cummings," *New Literary History* 18:3 (1987): 597–609.

Von Abele, Rudolph. "'Only to Grow': Change in the Poetry of E.E. Cummings," *PMLA* 70 (1955): 913–933.

Welch, Regis L. "The Linguistic Paintings of E. E. Cummings, Painter-Poet," *Language and Literature* 9:1 (1984): 79–89.

Wegner, Robert E. *The Poetry and Prose of E. E. Cummings*. New York: Harcourt, Brace & World, 1965.

West, Philip J. "Medieval Style and the Concerns of Modern Criticism," *College English* 34:6 (1973): 784–90.

Young, Robin V., ed. "E. E. Cummings 1894–1962," *Poetry Criticism* 5 (1992): 68–112.

ACKNOWLEDGMENTS

"Cummings' 'All in Green My Love Went Riding'" by Barry Sanders. From *The Explicator* Vol. XXV, No. 3, November 1966. Reprinted with permission of the Helen Dwight Reid Educational Foundation. Published by Heldref Publications, 1319 Eighteenth St., NW, Washington, DC 20036-1802. Copyright © 1966.

"Cummings' 'All in Green My Love Went Riding'" by William V. Davis. From *Concerning Poetry* 3, No. 2 (1970): 65–67. Copyright © 1970 by William V. Davis. Reprinted with permission.

"Memorabilia" by Clyde S. Kilby. From *The Explicator* Vol. XII, No. 2, November 1953. Reprinted with permission of the Helen Dwight Reid Educational Foundation. Published by Heldref Publications, 1319 Eighteenth St., NW, Washington, DC 20036-1802. Copyright © 1953.

"All in Green Went My Love Riding" by Cora Robey. From *The Explicator* Vol. XXVII, No. 10, November 1966. Reprinted with permission of the Helen Dwight Reid Educational Foundation. Published by Heldref Publications, 1319 Eighteenth St., NW, Washington, DC 20036-1802. Copyright © 1966.

"All in Green Went My Love Went Riding'" by Will C. Jumper. From *The Explicator* Vol. XXVI, No. 10, November 1969. Reprinted with permission of the Helen Dwight Reid Educational Foundation. Published by Heldref Publications, 1319 Eighteenth St., NW, Washington, DC 20036-1802. Copyright © 1969.

"Memorablia" by H. Seth Finn. From *The Explicator* Vol. XXIX, No. 10, June 1971. Reprinted with permission of the Helen Dwight Reid Educational Foundation. Published by Heldref Publications, 1319 Eighteenth St., NW, Washington, DC 20036-1802. Copyright © 1971.

"Memorablia" by Cynthia Barton. From *The Explicator* Vol. XXII, No. 4, December 1963. Reprinted with permission of the Helen Dwight Reid Educational Foundation. Published by Heldref Publications, 1319 Eighteenth St., NW, Washington, DC 20036-1802. Copyright © 1963.

Themes and Ideas